BENEFACTORS OF THE WORLD

BENEFACTORS
OF THE WORLD

By I. O. EVANS

Drawings by
George Craig

FREDERICK WARNE & CO. LTD.
LONDON AND NEW YORK

© FREDERICK WARNE & CO LTD
LONDON, ENGLAND
1968

ACKNOWLEDGMENTS

Thanks are given to Messrs Cassell & Co. Ltd, for permission to derive material for the section on Samuel Plimsoll from *The Plimsoll Mark* by David Masters. They are also given to the Royal National Institute for the Blind; to the Post Office Records Department of the General Post Office; to the Shaftesbury Society; to Dr Barnardo's Homes; to the British Red Cross Society; to the Carnegie Dunfermline Trust and the Carnegie United Kingdom Trust; to the Press Officer of the Salvation Army; and to the Perkins School for the Blind, Watertown, Mass., U.S.A., for help in compiling the sections relating to their work. For advice on the section on Sir Winston Churchill I am indebted to Mr Bernard Newman.

I.O.E.

LIBRARY OF CONGRESS CATALOG
CARD NO. 68–16853

7232   0918   9

Printed in Great Britain by
Cox & Wyman Ltd, London, Reading and Fakenham

433.1067

Contents

Introduction

Inventors of the World and *Engineers of the World,* two books similar to this, described some of the mechanical and electrical devices which have affected our lives during the past two centuries. This book tells of some of the changes which took place in social history over the same period, often as a result of the works mentioned in the previous books.

It is difficult to comprehend why people opposed such advances as enabling the blind to read by touch or the provision of safety for ships and sailors; yet even in our enlightened times we are often slow to accept revolutionary ideas, for it was only a few years ago that leading scientists ridiculed the idea of space travel.

In the nineteenth century people were much more class-conscious than they are today. The sentiment was a result of the feudal system about which you have probably read in history books. The poor who worked in mines and factories were regarded as inferior except by a few who were not afraid to try to bring improvement to working and domestic conditions.

In order to achieve their aims such reformers needed public support so that the authorities would take action; how, for instance, could General Booth have succeeded without the officers and soldiers of the Salvation Army, or Baden Powell without his Scouters and Guiders, his Scouts and Guides? Rowland Hill and Samuel Plimsoll had to work very strenuously indeed to make their ideals known before stamps were placed on envelopes and the load-line painted on ships.

Before they could succeed, these reformers had to arouse public opinion, to win the sympathy and active help of intelligent and bene-volent people. You will see in the following pages just what public opinion can do.

It did so much to make the world a better place that a new idea came into the public mind, the idea of 'progress'. Unfortunately this is easy to misunderstand; the world does not improve because of some mysterious force called 'progress': the progress comes because public-spirited people work for it, or at least support the active workers. Thoughtful adults regard it as a duty and a privilege to work for their ideals.

The first duty of you younger people for whom this book is written is to make the most of your education, not only to fit you to earn your living but also to enable you to form your own opinions so that you can decide which of the modern organisations and movements you wish to support. Meanwhile it may help you to read about the public-spirited people who did so much to make improvements; how they set about the task, overcame difficulties and were determined to succeed despite opposition and disappointments.

'Let us now praise famous men', were the words of the ancient religious book *Ecclesiasticus*, and they are still applicable two thousand years later.

If you want to do something practical, why not join the British Junior Red Cross, Scouts or Guides, or any other group of voluntary social workers?

I. O. E.

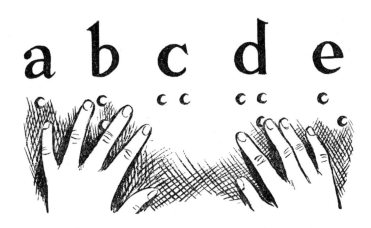

Reading by Touch

LOUIS BRAILLE
(1809–1852)

No decent person, today, would hurt or play spiteful tricks on a blind man; most people would gladly help him if they could. In the past, however, it was very different; a blind person was often resented as a burdensome nuisance, incapable of doing any useful work, and a butt for any unfeeling oaf. Heartless folk laughed to see the blind blundering about and colliding with things, and even put obstacles in their way for the fun of watching them fall. Indeed, when a tournament for the blind was held in Paris during the Middle Ages, crowds flocked to enjoy the sight of the victims aimlessly slashing at one another.

Yet there have always been people with sight who strove to help the afflicted, and many blind people who were able to earn their own living by skill in such handicrafts as basket-making. There have also been blind people who were not only brilliantly gifted but were given a chance to use their gifts. Some became renowned as musicians, thinkers or statesmen; and one of them did especially good work for those handicapped like himself.

Louis Braille was born on 4th January 1809 in Coupvray, a small village about twenty miles east of Paris. He was so very frail at birth that his parents feared he would never thrive and had him baptised when he was only four days old. He did thrive, however, and became healthy and lively.

When he was about three he wandered into the workshop of his father, who was the village saddler. Here there were attractive shining tools with which he wanted to play and pleasant-smelling pieces of leather that he could cut into shape, just as his father did. When nobody was looking he picked up a keen-edged saddler's knife and a piece of leather and started to cut, but the leather was tough and suddenly the knife slipped and its sharp, curved point pierced Louis's eye.

Had he been able to receive skilled treatment at once, the accident might not have been too serious, but unfortunately his well-meaning parents simply applied first-aid. After placing a cold compress on the eye they asked the village 'wise woman', who had a reputation as a healer, to bathe it with some herbal decoction. This stopped the bleeding and seemed to ease the pain so they did not trouble to consult the doctor, but soon they were horrified to see that Louis's eyes were becoming inflamed. Ophthalmia had set in, and, perhaps because the poor child could not be kept from rubbing his eyes, the infection had spread to both.

In those days there were no such drugs as penicillin and when the parents, now seriously alarmed, consulted the local doctors it was too late. Both eyes became increasingly bloodshot and Louis's sight got steadily worse. After a few days all he could see was the dim outline of the window and soon he could not even see that.

Distressed though his parents were, they did not make the mistake of treating him as a helpless invalid; they taught him to do odd jobs about the house and to cut the leather into fringes for the harness. He used to listen to, and join in the talk he heard round him, but before long his young life became confused and he was frightened by the sound of trampling hoofs and of harsh voices shouting words he could not understand. Napoleon had been defeated, and Russian and German troops had been quartered on Coupvray. Unwelcome as this enemy occupation was, however, it did bring work to the Braille household, for the troopers kept bringing their harness in for repair, and when, after about two years, it ceased the village became as peaceful as before.

Louis was so bright a boy that people took an interest in him. The local priest, while giving him religious instruction, taught him music and explained how to distinguish the songs of the birds. The village schoolmaster admitted him to his classes, which was very unusual for a blind child, and was delighted to find him a brilliant scholar. Whereas the other pupils could read the facts up later, if they were inattentive during a lesson, Louis had to pay attention and not merely to understand everything he heard but to commit it to memory. He even learned to remember the shapes of the letters of the alphabet, for his father 'wrote' them on a plank by driving round-headed nails into it so that he could recognise them by touch.

Soon Louis made such progress that some influential friends thought that he deserved a proper education, and they were able to arrange his admission to a special school for the blind in Paris.

Over thirty years previously a French civil servant, Valentin Haüy, had heard a group of blind players scraping untunefully on their violins. He had been horrified to see that they were absurdly dressed and that the crowd was jeering at them. This gave him an interest in blind welfare, and when he saw a sightless but intelligent-looking six-year-old boy begging outside a church he befriended him and taught

3

him to play musical instruments and to recite. By proving that the blind could be educated, he persuaded the authorities to open a special school in Paris for their benefit, *L'Institution National des Jeunes Aveugles*. It was to this school that Louis had been admitted.

It was a trying experience for Louis Braille, now eleven years old, when in 1819 his father took him by coach to Paris. He was jolted over rough roads and later was surrounded by the unfamiliar and rather alarming sounds and smells of a great city. He regretted leaving his quiet home and realised that for some time he would be parted from his family and friends. Louis cheered up, however, when he was given his school uniform of trousers, waistcoat, jacket with engraved buttons, and tall hat, and plunged into the middle of a geography lesson. Now that there was something for him to learn he felt more at home; he listened so attentively that he was able to give clear answers when the master questioned him, so he made a good start in his new life.

Conditions in the school were far from perfect: the building was damp and unhealthy, and there was even a shortage of water. Discipline was strict and punishments harsh, and the principal was inconsiderate and stern.

In spite of this, Louis Braille settled down fairly happily in his new life. The other pupils were mostly good comrades and one, Gabriel Gauthier, became his lifelong friend. The boys were given physical exercises and encouraged to play games, and once a week they were led, all holding on to a rope, to that well-known park the Jardin des Plantes, where they had more room to move.

Moreover, they were taught to play musical instruments, and Louis soon showed that he was a born musician, with a real gift for playing the piano and organ. There were also interesting handicrafts such as slipper-making, and for a boy of his intelligence school work was not a hardship but a delight. Before long he was gaining prizes, even in competition with pupils older than himself, and he also became a sort of monitor or pupil-teacher, first memorising the lessons and then teaching what he had learned to the other boys.

He was able to study a number of subjects: arithmetic and algebra, geography and history, and not only his own language, French, but the rudiments of English, Latin and Greek. Reading was taught by a method which Haüy had devised from books printed with embossed

4

letters, but as the letters had to be about three inches high in order to be recognisable, the books were heavy and cumbersome; there were so few books and they were so brief that some of the boys had learned them by heart. Writing was taught almost as clumsily by means of a 'writing-frame', but despite such difficulties Louis composed essays, the brilliance of which surprised his masters.

They especially impressed the new director, Dr Pignier, who had been appointed in 1821 to take charge of the school. Braille's essays, he said, were remarkable for exact thinking and for clear and correct language, and though they showed a vivid imagination, it was always controlled by good judgment.

Pignier was not so strict as his predecessor, and under his kind and sympathetic guidance the life of the pupils became far more pleasant. Hardly had he been appointed than he invited Valentin Haüy, through whose efforts the institution had been founded, to pay it a visit.

Haüy, now seventy-six years of age, accepted gladly and was given a great reception. The classrooms were decorated in his honour, the pupil's relations and friends were asked to be present, the boys recited, the school orchestra played and the school choir rendered a cantata which had been specially dedicated to him.

Deeply moved, Haüy spent the day with the boys, admiring their handiwork, sharing their meals, talking to them and meeting their families. At the end of his visit, when he was expected to make a speech describing how he had founded the institution; he simply said: 'It was God who did everything.'

Louis Braille was equally moved, and when the old man shook his hand and said a few encouraging words he was too excited to reply; but he made up his mind that he, like Haüy, would dedicate his life to helping the blind.

A few days later, when he went home for the holidays, he set to work. 'We blind are the loneliest people on earth,' he explained to his father. 'We can tell the different birds by their song and find our way about with our sticks, but without books we can never really learn.' The first problem was to devise some way of enabling them to read.

The method his father had used, of driving round-headed nails into a plank, might teach the blind their letters, but it was too clumsy for general use. He wanted something simpler and he realised that there was no need to copy the actual letters; it would be enough to use signs each representing a letter, so long as these were clear and easy to recognise. He experimented by cutting leather into slips and knocking small nails into pieces of wood. 'Listen to Louis pecking away,' the villagers said, half sympathetic and half amused.

Other thinkers had been working on the same problem, but some of their methods were not very practical; one consisted of patterns formed by sticking pins into a cushion, points upwards, for blind readers to feel! The trouble was that people who could see always found it hard to realise the special difficulties of the blind.

One thinker, however, had hit on a practical method. During the Napoleonic Wars an artillery officer, Captain Charles Barbier, had worked out an ingenious scheme for issuing orders during night operations. Using a punch to produce raised dots on a piece of card, he could give urgent commands, 'Advance!' 'Retire!' and so forth, that could be read by touch in the dark.

After the war Barbier realised that his system of 'night writing' could be adapted for use by the blind, and he had invented an ingenious little writing-frame for impressing the dots on to the card. Unfortunately his method was rather complicated, needing two vertical lines with up to six dots in each, and to make matters worse he based it not on ordinary spelling but on the sounds of the words. For this reason he called his method *Sonography*.

In spite of its defects, sonography was a great advance on any method so far devised, and after some difficulty and delay Barbier persuaded Dr Pignier to let the Institution give it a trial. The boys welcomed it enthusiastically; they were able to use it not only in their school work but to write personal notes to their friends.

Yet good as it was, the system had the usual fault of having been designed by a person with sight who did not fully understand a blind reader's problems. Braille, who understood them only too well from bitter experience, studied sonography and tried to improve it, and soon he was suggesting changes that made it easier to use. Far from being offended, Barbier welcomed them, though he must have been taken aback when he heard that they had been devised not by one of the Institution's staff but by a schoolboy in his teens!

Braille was not satisfied simply to introduce small improvements; he

realised that to be fit for general use sonography would have to be completely transformed. He worked at it by day during the intervals of
study, by night when the other boys in his dormitory were asleep, and
during his holidays in Coupvray. 'Well, Louis! Still at it, pecking
away?' the villagers chaffed him, though they were impressed by his
earnestness.

One fault, Braille realised, was that sonography was based on
sounds; it ought to be based on ordinary spelling. Another was that it
used so many dots that these had to be counted; he overcame this
defect by modifying the Barbier writing-frame so as to divide the dots
into two groups. When there were no more than three dots in a line he
found that there was no longer any need to count them: they formed
recognisable patterns which, with a little practice, could be distinguished at a touch.

Though this gave him an idea of what a successful blind alphabet
could be, actually working it out was very difficult, and naturally he
made mistakes which he had to correct. He tried using short dashes as
well as dots, but found that though they were easy to read they were

difficult to impress on the paper. After much thought and effort he devised a scheme which really worked.

He used varying combinations of raised dots in an oblong three dots high and two dots wide, and found that this gave him a total of sixty-three possible combinations whereas Barbier's method gave only thirty-six.

```
1 *     4 *
2 *     5 *
3 *     6 *
```

Working through the alphabet, Braille represented letter A by dot 1, B by dots 1 and 2, C by 1 and 4, and so on, until he reached Z, dots 1, 3, 5, and 6; the remaining signs were used for punctuation marks and mathematical signs. Though some of these groups might be confused, most, as he verified for himself, were quite easy to recognise by touch.

At this time he was only about twenty-two years old!

Though later workers have improved his system, it is still in principle the method devised by Louis Braille, and it is always called after him.

Barbier was not at all annoyed at finding his own system superseded by the Braille. On the contrary, he congratulated its inventor very warmly, and Braille responded by saying how much his system owed to Barbier's sonography, which had made him realise the lines on which to work.

The pupils in the Institution wanted to have some method of reading music by touch, so Braille adapted his system to meet their needs.

So excellent was the system that he had invented, and so eagerly did his comrades welcome it, that he might have expected the Institution to bring it into use at once. Instead, to his great distress, they forbade it, insisting that the Haüy system, using embossed letters of the ordinary alphabet, should be the only one taught. It was not that they wanted to be harsh or obstructive – far from it; they simply thought that it was a sad waste of time for blind people to have an alphabet of their own which nobody else could read.

Despite their orders, however, the pupils went on using Braille so long as nobody in authority was present, and when some of the instructors realised what was happening they did not interfere. Thus the boys were able to take notes during their lessons with the aid of metal slates, until they had so many pages of Braille notes that they were like small text-books which they could read by touch. At last the system came into general use within the Institution and gradually spread outside.

While he was developing his system Louis Braille was appointed a junior master. He accepted the position with some reluctance, for his real wish was to become a professional musician, but he nevertheless thought it his duty to devote his life to the blind. This meant some personal sacrifice, too, for as an assistant master he was not very generously paid. He still wore the Institution uniform, distinguished only by a special badge; like the boys he could not leave the premises or receive visitors without permission, and he was punished if he broke the rules. On the other hand, he had his own little bedroom instead of having to sleep in the dormitory, which gave him more privacy for his work, though he missed the company of his friend Gauthier.

Realising Braille's love of music, Pignier sometimes invited him to play at evening parties outside the Institution, but except for the opportunity they gave him of playing the piano, he did not much enjoy them. The noise wearied him and the idle chatter bored him, and although his audience applauded and praised his talent, he could not help thinking that some of them did not care for music at all and that their admiration was mingled with a feeling of condescending pity for 'that poor blind man'.

His reputation spread not merely through Paris but to other lands, and he was consulted by an Austrian professor who wished to teach the blind to read and write. But unfortunately the professor did not approve of the Braille system, for the usual reason – that nobody except the blind could use it. Later Braille was invited to go to Vienna to teach a young prince who had lost his sight, but he refused: it was his task to devote himself not to one blind person but to the blind.

Realising that there was some force in the objection that few people with sight could read his system, he tried to work out a method which both they and the blind could use. He devised what he called *Raphigraphy*, a method of 'dotting in' the outlines of the ordinary letters; and a blind inventor constructed a machine, something like a crude forerunner of the typewriter, by which these dots could be impressed. Braille also adapted his writing-frame so that a blind man could trace the ordinary letters in a recognisable form.

9

The French Government at last acknowledged that the building in which the Institution was housed was cramped and unhealthy, and transferred it in 1843 to larger and more suitable premises in a more salubrious quarter of Paris. By this time, however, Braille's health had been ruined by the dampness and stale air in which he had lived for so long. He had developed tuberculosis. In those days there was no cure for this, and though the director relieved him of some of his duties and allowed him long holidays in the fresh air of Coupvray, it was too late. Sometimes he seemed to be recovering, and at one time he actually believed that he was cured, but the disease returned and he accepted the possibility that he was doomed to an early death.

His religious beliefs were too sincere for him to be dismayed, and he refused to be deceived when his friends tried to buoy him up with false hopes. 'You know you can't pay me with that sort of coinage,' he replied gently. 'You don't have to pretend.'

On 6th January 1852, just after his forty-third birthday, Louis Braille prepared for death as methodically as if he were going on a journey. In his will he remembered all those who had helped him, from the Institution itself to the servant who had cleaned his room. He received Holy Communion, and as it was the Feast of the Epiphany he asked to be reminded of the religious meaning of the gifts, gold, frankincense and myrrh, which the Three Wise Men had brought to the Christ-child. He bade farewell to his friends, and when he could no longer speak he was still able to smile at them.

Among his belongings was a box marked 'To be destroyed unopened after my death'. It was opened, however, and was found to contain a record of the loans he had made; destroying this would cancel all the debts due to him.

Although he was dead, his work continued, for his system was adopted throughout the world. In England, as elsewhere, several different methods of reading by touch had come into use, and blind readers who had learned one were quite unable to read books or letters written in another. Owing largely to the efforts of Dr Armitage, who himself was blind, this difficulty was overcome. With three colleagues – also blind – he made a careful study of all the methods and came to the conclusion that Braille's was easily the best.

The organisation he founded, the English Braille Publishing House, has now become the Royal National Institute for the Blind. Though it also uses the Moon system, based on simplified forms of the ordinary letters, for blind readers who find Braille too difficult, the bulk of its work is done in Braille's system. Together with the National Library for the Blind it publishes versions of many thousands of books on a wide variety of subjects, as well as Braille newspapers and magazines. It lends them to blind readers and supplies them with a Braille writer which is very easy to use, and has a special students' library of educational and other books.

The system which Braille devised for use in France needed very little adaptation for British readers. As there are no accented letters in English, the signs which correspond to them in French have been given other uses: some stand for very common words such as 'for' and 'the', others for common groups of letters such as 'th' and 'ed'. As some of the letters and other signs can also stand for words or punctuation marks, Braille is rather difficult to master, but none the less it is certainly the best method of reading by touch that has ever been devised.

Personally modest and retiring, Louis Braille is now recognised as one of the greatest of the world's benefactors, and years after his death

the French Government decided to pay him the honours he had neither received nor desired during his lifetime. In June 1952 his body was exhumed from its grave in peaceful Coupvray, and – apart from his hands, which were placed in a sealed urn and allowed to remain in the village – was removed to the Pantheon in Paris; except that it is not a religious building, this is the Westminster Abbey of France.

This second funeral procession was very impressive, not so much because of the military escort, the bands and the presence of members of the French Government and other famous men, but because of the hundreds of blind men, women and children who attended it. Some wearing dark glasses, and many feeling their way with white sticks or led by relatives and friends who could see, they followed the coffin from the Institution in which Braille had worked to the Pantheon and stood silent as, to the sound of solemn music, it was lowered into the crypt.

Whether Braille himself would have approved of such pomp and circumstance is doubtful; he might well have preferred that his body should rest undisturbed in the peaceful cemetery at Coupvray. He might, however, have been pleased to know that the farmhouse in which he had lived should now be a Louis Braille Museum, containing not only personal mementoes of himself but demonstrations of the many and widespread applications of his work.

The signposts which mark the route to Coupvray display a hand grasping a white stick and invite the traveller to visit Louis Braille's birthplace. Here, outside his former home, is a plaque which bears, in French and English, an inscription which would certainly have rejoiced his heart, for it contains the words:

'He opened the doors of knowledge to all those who cannot see.'

Welfare in the Factory

ROBERT OWEN
(1771–1858)

COTTON manufacture has always been mechanised: the spinning-wheel and loom are almost as old as civilisation. It was one of the first manufactures to be industrialised when in the eighteenth century a number of new machines were invented, including the spinning-mule and the power-loom.

Unlike the spinning-wheel and the hand-loom, the new machines could not be used in the workers' homes. Instead they were installed in great factories and tended by a number of 'hands' – not only men and women but even young children – who were underpaid, overworked, and harshly treated. Most of the mill-owners took these grim conditions for granted, thinking them the only way of making the industry 'pay', until at last one owner realised that they were unnecessary and evil.

Like Louis Braille, Robert Owen – born on 14th May 1771 in Newtown, mid Wales – was the son of a saddler, and he too was injured during his childhood; though the injury was not as dreadful as blindness, it was quite serious. A mouthful of scalding hot porridge, which he incautiously gulped down, so impaired his digestion that throughout his life he had to be very careful of what he ate. But this had a great effect upon his character: as he wrote later in his

13

Autobiography, it '. . . made me attend to the effects of different qualities of food on my changed constitution, and gave me the habit of close observation and of continual reflection.'

As Louis Braille would have been but for his blindness, young Robert Owen was a great reader, borrowing books from the town's educated men and usually completing one every day. When he was only seven he was appointed 'usher' (assistant master) in the local school until he found employment in a combined drapery and general store.

Yet he was no mere bookworm: he enjoyed dancing, played football and other strenuous games, and prided himself on being the best runner and long and high jumper in the school. He said later that when he tried to teach himself to play the clarinet he must have annoyed the whole neighbourhood.

Dissatisfied with life in Newtown, when he was eleven Robert Owen went to London where his eldest brother was working. After a period in a small drapery in Stamford, he was employed in a larger one on Old London Bridge. Here, however, conditions were so hard that he asked a friend to try to find a better situation for him. His working hours might be from eight in the morning until two next morning, with only brief breaks to snatch a hasty meal; and he had to have his hair elaborately curled and powdered and worked into a stiff pigtail. Yet his work gave him pleasant companionship; he had Sundays off; and when trade slackened he grew more reconciled. At last he forgot that he had ever wished for a different job, and was quite taken aback when he learned that his friend had found one for him.

His new situation was in a drapery in Manchester. That town was noted for the reforming zeal of its leading citizens and for their interest in science; the Manchester 'Lit. and Phil.' (Literary and Philosophical Society) had so great a reputation that it was a privilege to be a member.

Two years later Owen was approached by a man called Jones, who supplied the drapery with wire frames for ladies' bonnets. Jones was full of enthusiasm for the 'new and curious' machines used for spinning cotton, and said that if Owen could raise a hundred pounds they could go into business together, manufacturing these machines, and make their fortunes.

Owen borrowed the money from his brother in London and became Jones's partner, renting a workshop, buying the material needed and engaging forty men. Soon, however, he found that his new partner, whatever his knowledge of machinery, had no idea of running a business or controlling men. He, on the other hand, knew nothing about the machines, but by dint of walking about the factory watching everything and looking extremely wise, he at last mastered their use and the business began to prosper.

He was pleased when Jones, who wanted a richer partner, offered to 'buy him out' in return for six spinning-mules and some of the other machinery. True, Owen received only three of the mules, but these enabled him to set up business on his own account as a manufacturer of cotton thread.

Before long he heard one of his spinners say that Mr Drinkwater, a wealthy mill-owner, was looking for a new manager. Without hesitation he put on his hat and went to apply for the job.

'You are too young,' Drinkwater complained. 'How old are you?'

'Twenty,' Robert Owen told him.

'And how often do you get drunk in the week?' Drinkwater wanted to know, for drunkenness was very common then.

Owen blushed scarlet. 'I was never drunk in my life,' he declared.

This seemed to impress Drinkwater, who asked him what salary he wanted. Owen's answer astonished him. 'What?' he exclaimed. 'Three hundred pounds? I've had I don't know how many asking for this job, and I don't think that all they asked put together would amount to that.'

'I can't be governed by what others ask,' Owen declared, 'and I can't take less. I'm making that out of my own business.'

A cautious man, Drinkwater visited Owen's tiny factory, examined his account-books, and asked him for business references. Quite satisfied, he appointed him to take charge of his own factory, but did not tell him how large it was.

When Owen realised the size of the task he had undertaken his heart almost failed him. With no advice or instruction, for Drinkwater knew very little and the previous manager had left, he was now responsible for a factory full of unfamiliar machinery and employing five hundred workers!

Again he used his former method of inspecting everything, examining the plans of the machines, coming early and leaving late, and for the time being giving no orders but merely saying yes or no when he was asked anything, and looking as wise as he could. The knowledge of cotton goods he had gained in the drapery helped him, and he had a trick of getting the best out of his men; after six weeks he felt himself 'master of his position', in full control of the work and able to correct any defects in the machinery. A year later Drinkwater asked him to take charge of a spinning-factory at Northwich, so Owen became the manager of two separate businesses.

Though at first he felt shy and awkward, 'speaking ungrammatically a kind of Welsh-English and subject painfully to blushing', he gradually became more self-confident. He gained a reputation as an expert on fine-cotton spinning and was admitted to the Manchester 'Phil. and Lit.' where he could enjoy the company of many famous men.

For a time Owen shared rooms with a young artist who had become an engineer, and made him a generous loan to help him design a machine for excavating canals. Later in life he was glad and proud that he had given this help, for the young engineer was the Robert Fulton who became famous as the inventor of the submarine and steamship.*

*See *Inventors of the World*, pp. 63–76

About 1795 Owen parted company with Drinkwater and became manager of another large firm, being responsible not only for managing the mills but for buying the raw cotton and selling the finished material. During the next year, when he became a member of the Manchester Board of Health, he learned much about working conditions in the factories.

His work in finding markets for the goods his firm manufactured took him as far afield as Glasgow. There he was introduced to a young lady, Anne Caroline Dale, who must have liked him at once, for she immediately invited him to visit her father's mills, and a little later he heard, rather to his surprise, that she had said, 'I don't know how it is, but if ever I marry, he's to be my husband.' After they had met a few times he asked her, as was then the custom, whether 'her affections were engaged', a tactful way of proposing marriage; she replied, as was also the custom, that he must 'ask father', but she added that she felt very doubtful whether he would give her to a southerner whom he did not know.

But when Owen met her father what he asked for was not his daughter but his factory. For David Dale's spinning mills at New Lanark, about a mile and half from the historic town of Old Lanark and about thirty miles from Glasgow, were not merely flourishing; they were excellently run and were regarded as 'one of the most humanely conducted factories in the Empire'.

Dale, a kindly man, was especially noted for the care he gave to the children he employed. There were about five hundred of them, two hundred being under ten years old. They slept in airy rooms, were encouraged to wash before and after work, and had their clothes washed regularly; and though they worked thirteen hours a day, they had an hour and a half break for meals, and after their working hours they were educated. About eighty of them could read, twenty-eight of them fairly well.

Good though these conditions were, judged by the standards of the time, they did not satisfy Owen who made up his mind that if he ever became manager he would greatly improve them. First, however, he had to buy the mills, and like Drinkwater, their owner thought him too young for such a position (Owen was then twenty-seven). At last, however, Dale consented to sell, and even left it to Owen to fix a fair price.

So in the summer of 1799, an important date in the history of industrial relations in Britain, Robert Owen took over the New Lanark Mills.

In September of that year, he married Dale's daughter, Caroline, but he was astonished at the brevity of the marriage service in the Church of Scotland. As he described it later:

> Mr Balfour (the clergyman) requested Miss Dale and me to stand up, and asked each of us if we were willing to take the other for husband and wife, and each simply nodding assent, he said without one word more – "Then you are married and may sit down' – and the ceremony was all over.

Owen did not actually take up his duties as manager of New Lanark Mills until January 1800, one of his first acts being to refuse to engage any more young children, and to improve the working conditions of the others. It could not be supposed, he said, that children could work for thirteen hours a day, even with breaks for meals, and then be educated; many of them, he pointed out, 'become dwarfs in body and mind, and some of them are deformed'. So he resolved to make ten years the minimum age at which to employ them.

When it came to the older workers he had to be more cautious, for most of them, he complained, were ignorant and indolent 'and much addicted to theft, drunkenness and falsehood'. They regarded a Welshman as a foreigner, and found it hard to understand his accent. They were suspicious, too, of his new-fangled ideas, thinking that he was scheming to make them work harder, and when they heard that, unlike Dale, he was going to live nearby, they feared that this was so that he could spy on them. All he could do for the moment was to follow his usual plan of remaining silent but observant until he knew not only what needed to be done but how he could best set about doing it.

He scrapped the obsolete machines and replaced them by more modern types, and he rearranged them so as to get a steadier 'flow of work' through the factory. Finding that much theft and pilfering was taking place, he did not punish the offenders – he was no believer in punishment – but made thieving more difficult and easier to detect; he also gave hints on how money could be made more honestly.

To check slackness, he placed beside each worker a small wooden

tab, its four sides painted in different colours, which could be turned to indicate the worker's efficiency: when the black side was turned foremost it showed that the man was a bad worker; when blue that he was 'indifferent'; when yellow that he was good; and when white that he was excellent. Each worker's efficiency was also recorded in a book. This plan worked splendidly, and gradually fewer of the black and blue sides were to be seen and more of the yellow and white.

In spite of Owen's dislike of punishments there was one fault which he could not overcome in any other way. Drunkenness had been very common, but by imposing fines and by occasional dismissals, he succeeded in almost completely stamping it out. The fines, along with a small contribution (one eightieth) from each worker's wage, were paid into a sick-fund – there was of course no Health Insurance in those days – and the men were provided with free medical attention.

Owen's thoughtfulness for his workers at last overcame the prejudice they had felt against him. During a slack period when the mills had to shut down he arranged for them to be paid their full wages, which won their liking and respect.

Outside the factory he gave much attention to the town. Many of the houses in New Lanark, built by David Dale, had only one room and most were not merely dirty and neglected but badly damaged, for some of the tenants had used the window-shutters and doors as firewood. Outside almost every door was a rubbish-dump. Owen added another storey to the houses, giving an extra room. He had the rubbish-dumps moved away and the streets cleaned and paved.

In spite of his efforts some of the tenants were so feckless that they soon made the houses as dirty as ever, and neither good advice nor rules seemed to make any difference. Owen, however, persuaded them to appoint a committee whose duty it was to visit the houses every week and report on their condition. Though the men welcomed this idea, their wives did not; they called the visitors 'Bug Hunters' and refused to let them in. On Owen's advice the visitors did not force their way in, but simply announced the names of the women who kept their houses clean. That made the other women feel that, as people say nowadays, they ought to 'keep up with the Joneses' and earn praise for their own homes for cleanliness.

Finding that the shops in New Lanark had been selling inferior goods at high prices, Owen provided a company store which sold coal, food, and other necessities at very reasonable rates. In spite of its low prices, the store soon made a profit of about seven hundred pounds a year, which he devoted to the upkeep of a school for the workers' children. Thus, when his partners protested, he was able to assure them that the cost of the school did not come out of their pockets but was borne by the people themselves.

This did not satisfy the partners, who felt that their money was being squandered on welfare work, so they readily agreed when Owen offered to buy them out and form his own company for running the mills. But to his distress he found that his new partners were even less sympathetic; they wanted to 'freeze him out' of the company and to sell the mills.

What they did not realise was that Owen's plans were well known even outside the cotton industry, and that he now had wealthy friends, who, though not interested in manufacturing, were full of sympathy for his welfare work. To enable this to continue they willingly formed a partnership, bought the mills and reinstated him as manager.

In 1814, after this had been arranged, Owen was travelling home by carriage through Old Lanark and was amazed to see a crowd, including townspeople as well as factory hands from New Lanark, rushing towards him. Although he protested that the workers had been beasts of burden long enough, they insisted on unharnessing the horses and themselves hauling his carriage along. With a flag borne in front of him and a band playing, he was escorted home in triumph, while all the windows in New Lanark were lit up in his honour; and when he made a short speech of thanks he was given a hearty cheer. Delighted that his workers should think so highly of him, he said that it increased his determination to do them and their children all the good in his power.

With this end in view, he built what he called 'The Institute for the Formation of Character'. It included schools for the older children, a 'playground' like a nursery school for the younger children, an adult school, community rooms and public halls.

Owen's educational methods were as original as his plans for running a factory: when he forbade any sort of punishment in his school it must have surprised everyone! Though he knew the children would have to learn reading, writing and a little simple arithmetic, he had no faith in mere 'book learning', and he appointed as teachers a weaver who was not very well educated himself and a village girl of seventeen. The important quality that each should possess was 'having a way' with children, being fond of them, and being willing to co-operate in Owen's plans. He insisted that 'the children should never hear from their teachers an angry word or see a cross or threatening look,' for the school was a place to make them happy, as he strove to do himself.

'You love those children better than your own,' his wife Caroline protested. They had four sons and three daughters.

The children in the school were to learn not through books, which were mostly used for reference, but through talks and discussions, from the things around them, and from pictures, maps, a globe of the world and a 'time chart'. They were taught world history, geography and natural history, going out into the woods to collect specimens and study nature. Owen, who wanted the children to enjoy their schooling, had them taught to sing and dance, and to drill in the playground, barefoot and lightly clad, to the tune of a drum-and-fife band.

Such methods were so novel that the New Lanark schools became famous. People interested in education visited them from far away to see how they were run and were deeply impressed by their excellence. From Robert Owen's work came nursery and infant schools and other modern methods, and he preceded H. G. Wells in realising the importance of world, as opposed to national history.

Owen's success in his factory and his school gave him a great reputation as a social reformer. He sat for Parliament and was defeated only by a very narrow margin. He tried to have an act passed regulating the hours of child labour in factories and although he did not then succeed, his efforts prepared the way for the Factory Acts which came into force later.

His reputation spread overseas, and when in 1818 he visited Europe he was welcomed and 'lionised' by educationalists, political thinkers, scientists and rulers. But though many people realised the value of his methods, others did not. 'If the common people,' one politician shocked him by asking, 'get wealthy and independent of us, how are we to govern them?'

Owen's aim was to make the common people more wealthy and independent; he had already been consulted on plans for overcoming poverty, and on his return to Britain he proposed a scheme for bringing prosperity to Lanarkshire. It included town-planning, with a Green Belt between the factories and the villages and central heating in the houses. It startled many people, in days when over-dressing was usual, by suggesting that clothing should be simple, healthy and cheap.

By now Owen's partners thought that he was going rather too far, so they bought him out of the company and arranged for his mills and his schools to be run by someone else. He did not mind greatly, for he was anxious to proceed with his scheme for town-planning. In those days America was the great land of opportunity, where new towns were always being built and new ideas were welcome; it was the ideal place for projects such as his.

A flourishing community, Harmony in Indiana, had been formed by a religious group who now wanted to move to another site and were offering it for sale. With his family's full approval, Owen decided to purchase it and to run it on his own lines, hoping to make it into an ideal society of unselfish people, all working together for the common good. When he had proved that this could be done, he believed that other similar communities would be organised, and so the world would gradually be transformed.

When in 1824 he emigrated to America he was welcomed by many celebrities, including the President and some Indian chiefs. Taking

control in the following year of what he now called New Harmony, he invited 'industrious and well-disposed people of all nations' to join in forming a community.

Unfortunately he seemed to have lost his business ability and commonsense, giving a welcome to all-comers without making sure whether or not they were really 'industrious and well-disposed'. Some were, and with their aid the community flourished – for a time. But there were so many others, some useless and some harmful, that after a few years he had to abandon the idea.

Though the community, after Owen's return to England in 1829, was no longer run on the lines he had hoped for, it became an educational centre. It had passed largely under the control of his four sons, and when one of them, David Dale Owen, was appointed United States Geologist, it became the headquarters of the U.S. Geological Survey. So, though it had not fulfilled his hopes, Robert Owen's work at New Harmony could not be called fruitless.

Disappointed but not discouraged, Owen was no sooner back in England than he began to spread his ideals anew. Now, however, he had very different problems to face, and a very different public to influence.

He was no longer the wealthy manager and part-owner of a prosperous factory and a flourishing school. He was comparatively poor, for he had lost much of his wealth in New Harmony, and he was thought to be rather eccentric and even something of a revolutionary, so new and startling were many of his ideas.

Wealthy influential people were not so ready to listen to him, for though he was still regarded as an authority on factory reform and schools, his ideals of community were a different matter. Apart from anything else he talked at such length that many people got bored and stopped paying any attention to him, but none the less he was so sincere that they still liked and admired him.

Though he had lost his old public, however, he had gained a new one. The poorer people, the workers, knew of his hopes for improving their living conditions, and they knew that he did not, like so many others, look down on them or try to patronise them. Even when they found him too difficult to work with, they were still heartened by his example and his teaching; as one of them told him, 'Your doctrines have made me a better and happier being'. So they found their own ways of striving to make a practical use of his ideals.

They made many attempts, for example, to form co-operative societies. At first these were failures, until in 1855 a small group of Lancashire weavers found the proper way to run them. From the small 'co-op' they opened in Toad Lane, Rochdale, came the great co-operative movements of modern times; and still, like those Rochdale Pioneers, the modern co-operators know how much they owe to the ideals of Robert Owen. Some of the modern societies, too, are not merely trading concerns; they carry out educational work of which he would have heartily approved.

He tried many unsuccessful schemes: for basing money on work instead of on gold; for running a National Labour Exchange; for organising the Grand National Consolidated Trades Union, to which all the workers would belong. He tried to form another community, Harmony Hall, in Hampshire, but, in much the same way as New Harmony in Indiana, it failed after a promising start and became a college.

Unperturbed by failure after failure, Owen kept on endeavouring to spread his ideas. He wrote books, edited papers, travelled in Britain and abroad lecturing, and started to compile his *Autobiography*. About 1853, when he was over eighty, he became a spiritualist.

When, in 1858, he wished to make a public address, he was so feeble that he had to be carried to the hall in a sedan chair and lifted on to the platform. Hardly had he begun to speak than a friend, taking pity on his weakness, started a round of applause as though he had finished and said, 'Capital, very good; can't be better, Mr Owen. There, that will do.' Then he added quietly, 'Take the old gentleman back to his bed.'

Though he collapsed on reaching his home, Owen was well enough a fortnight later to travel to Newtown, and when he crossed the boundary between England and Wales, he sat up in his carriage and gave a cheer. On the day before he died he made plans for holding a series of meetings in the town and for reorganising the education of the parish.

He died on 17th November 1858, and was buried in Newtown's old churchyard, where, in 1902, a bronze plaque, bought by subscription from the co-operators of Great Britain, was placed on the iron railings of his tomb. It shows Robert Owen, with the veiled figure of Justice behind him, greeting a number of workers bowed down under the weight of the burdens they bear.

Many of his schemes had failed, and he did not live to see the better conditions which he helped to bring about, but in spite of repeated failure, he had shown the value of welfare work in the factory, of kindness in the schools, and he continued to work undaunted almost to the end of his life. Not only the Co-operative Movement but the Trade Unions and many other organisations owe much to him, and he inspired many of our ideals. These are summed up in a sentence from his teachings which is quoted on his tomb:

> It is the one great and universal interest of the human race to be cordially united, and to aid each other to the full extent of their capacities.

Not yet is the human race cordially united, but some of Robert Owen's hopes have been fulfilled in the modern Welfare State for which he helped to prepare the way.

The Penny Post

ROWLAND HILL
(1795–1879)

THE British postal service has long been a government monopoly, people who tried to infringe it being liable to prosecution. In the old days letters were collected and carried about the country, and although they were not usually delivered there were arrival points from which they could be collected. Yet the methods used were very different from those of today.

The postal charges were heavy, and based partly on distance, partly on weight, and partly on the number of sheets of paper in the letter; twice as much was charged for two very small sheets as one large enough to weigh an ounce. Envelopes were seldom used, for they would cost as much as an extra sheet; instead the paper was folded and secured with sealing-wax. To make certain that the letter contained only the one sheet of paper, the postal officials used to 'candle' it, by holding it up to a strong light; if a banknote were enclosed in a letter this would be seen, so most people, rather than run the risk of their money being stolen, would cut it in half and send the two halves separately.

The further a letter had to be carried, the greater was the charge. To send it to another address in the same town cost only a penny; and although pennies were worth more than they are now that was a reasonable amount. To send it only fifteen miles, however, cost fourpence, and the rates from London to Wolverhampton, to Glasgow and to Aberdeen were respectively 10d, 1s 3½d and 1s 4½d – the odd halfpenny for Scotland being the toll paid when a letter was sent across the Border. Rates for destinations abroad were of course higher.

The charge was made not when the letter was collected but when it was delivered to the person to whom it was addressed; and if the addressee were unable or unwilling to pay the postage, the letter was not delivered at all. This meant that many poor people, who simply could not afford to pay these heavy rates, were quite unable to receive letters from distant relatives or friends; they might even have to refuse a letter even though they realised that it contained important or serious news.

To make things worse, many wealthy and influential people did not have to pay any postal charges at all. Members of Parliament, among others, were entitled to 'frank' their letters by simply writing their names on them, and then no charge whatever was made for postage. Moreover, they could transfer the same privilege to their friends, and as some of them habitually did this, the Post Office incurred a great loss of revenue.

Such people might not have been concerned because high postal rates prevented poor people from keeping in touch with their relatives and friends, but when they found that these rates were hindering trade and manufacture, they realised that the service would have to be reorganised. Many suggestions were made for improving the postal service, but little action was taken until a method was devised for its complete transformation.

Rowland Hill, born at Kidderminster on 3rd December 1795, was even more incapacitated during his early childhood than Louis Braille; he was threatened with spinal trouble, and for some years had to spend much time lying down. This did not stop him thinking, however, and he day-dreamed of accomplishing something to improve his country, thus making his life worth while.

Eventually however, he recovered and was able to join in his brother's activities: carpentry and metalwork at their own forge. Rowland, who had a deep interest in science, constructed an electrical machine, mapped a stretch of the countryside and developed a life-long enthusiasm for astronomy.

When his father became headmaster of Hill Top School, Birmingham, he and two of his brothers helped to run it, sometimes studying a lesson on their way to school in order to be able to teach it when they arrived. Some years later, Rowland became headmaster, and when the school was moved to Hazelwood (also in Birmingham) he designed the new buildings himself.

He and his brothers, who had learned from their parents to value freedom and to hate any sort of tyranny, tried to apply these ideals in their school, as far as possible, allowing the boys to help run it, and at a time when corporal punishment was usual, they completely abolished the use of the cane and birch. Their methods were as original and attracted as much attention as those of Robert Owen. Many people came to study the 'Hazelwood system' of education and were deeply impressed.

The pupils were encouraged to develop their special talents by the availability of the school's own roof-top observatory and laboratory, well equipped with engineering models and scientific instruments. They learned drawing and etching, and printed and illustrated the school magazine by means of the school printing presses. They produced their own plays and acted them in the school theatre, and they played in the school band.

Rowland Hill, who was a brilliant artist, painted the scenery for the theatre but on one occasion his artistic gifts almost caused him serious trouble: when he was seen painting Dover Castle during the Napoleonic Wars, he was mistaken for a spy! It was not this, however, but sheer pressure of work which later made him give up his painting, although he never lost his love of art.

He continued as headmaster when the school was transferred to Bruce Castle, Tottenham, where he proceeded to run it on the same lines as at Hazelwood. The famous author De Quincy praised it highly; he said that unlike most other schools it cultivated happiness as well as knowledge; indeed, it was a place where even a timid boy could be happy, which was then very unusual.

Although he found Robert Owen too difficult a person to work with, Rowland Hill was greatly interested in his plans for communities and had, at one time, considered joining New Harmony. In 1832 he suggested a scheme for overcoming poverty and reducing crime by establishing 'Home Colonies' where poor people could cultivate the waste lands of Britain instead of emigrating to those overseas.

In 1835 he invented a machine for printing, with revolving cylinders, on to a continuous roll of paper, but although this worked extremely well, it did not come into general use until it was tried again years later by someone else.

Having resigned the headmastership of Bruce Castle School, Hill became secretary to the Colonisation Commissioners for South Australia. Part of his duty was to ensure that the emigrant ships were seaworthy and suited for a long voyage, and although some of the ship-owners at first protested, his work helped to make them comply.

While he was inspecting one of these ships he noticed a certain Devon farmer who had such an eager look that he remarked, 'I feel sure that man will do well.' Many years later, when that emigrant returned to England, he gave Hill a fine gold nugget; he had been poor when he

went out, he explained, but those words had given him fresh heart and spurred him on to success.

At last, however, Rowland Hill felt that his duty lay in attempting to reform the postal service, and thenceforward he devoted the majority of his time to that task. He had already joined an association formed to abolish such 'taxes on knowledge' as the stamp-duty which newspapers had to pay; this had been imposed only as a war-tax but although the country had been at peace for twenty years it was still enforced. He pointed out that if this tax were reduced the Government would lose nothing because more newspapers would be sold and this would encourage advertising and trade.

He realised, however, that something more far-reaching than a mere reduction of the stamp duty on newspapers was required: the whole postal service needed to be run on different lines. Some years previously he had suggested two schemes, both of which have since shown their value, although they were not put into practice at the time. One was a 'travelling post-office', rather like those now in use but travelling not by railways but on the roads – a mail-coach specially fitted-up so that the guard could sort and date-stamp the letters while it was actually moving; the other was for sending small letters through pneumatic tubes, similar to those now used in Paris.

Foremost among the other thinkers who had been working on postal reform was Robert Wallace, M.P. for Greenock. When he heard of Rowland Hill's plans he offered to give him all the help he could, and sent him a cab-load of Parliamentary 'Blue Books' containing statistics and other useful information about the postal service. Fortunately as a Member of Parliament he was able to frank this half-hundredweight of material and send it free, for the cost of postage would have been ruinous!

Hill's brothers also helped him a great deal; indeed when he had worked out his scheme in detail his eldest brother, Matthew, advised him to have it printed in pamphlet form and suggested a suitable publisher. When it appeared in 1837 Rowland Hill was careful to avoid calling it 'Penny Postage', because it seemed so absurd an idea that people's minds would be turned against it, so it appeared under the more modest title *Post Office Reform: Its Importance and Practicability*.

He began by pointing out that whenever taxes had been reduced, for example on soap, silk goods or coffee, the prices of these goods had fallen, and the lower prices had led to a great increase in sales. Surely, then, if more of the taxes were reduced, trade would prosper so much that the lower taxes would bring in more revenue to the Government. The important aim was to find out which of the taxes should be reduced in order to give the greatest help to the people with as little loss as possible to the revenue.

He then quoted figures to show that although the population of Britain had increased greatly during the last twenty years, the revenue from its postal service had actually fallen slightly, whereas that of France had almost doubled. Plainly there was something gravely wrong with the service.

Even more serious than the loss of revenue was the high cost of correspondence, which hindered trade and caused much unnecessary hardship and distress. If, on the other hand, the postal service were reformed, it would cease to impose an unbearable tax on the country and would help to civilise it.

Then he gave details. Using the information he had gained from the Blue Books, he showed that the average cost to the Post Office of handling one letter was just over four-fifths of a penny. Of this only about a third was the cost of actually conveying the letter from place to place; the rest was spent in receiving the letter at one post office and allowing it to be collected from another. Moreover, if the cost of bulky newspapers and franked postal packets were taken into account, the actual cost of handling one ordinary letter was a tenth of a penny!

The total cost of a journey by mail-coach from London to Edinburgh was five pounds, about 16s 8d per hundredweight. As the usual weight of a letter was about a quarter of an ounce, the cost of conveying each letter was only one thirty-sixth of a penny; yet the postage for this journey on even the very lightest letter, consisting of one small sheet of paper, was 1s 3½d!

Then Rowland Hill had an idea which was so novel that it startled himself as much as it did others: the charge made on a letter should depend neither on the number of sheets of paper it contained nor even on the distance it had to be carried, but simply on its weight. Then there would no longer be any need to waste time 'candling' the letters, or working out how far they had to go; it would only be necessary to weigh them.

Moreover, if postage were paid before the letters were sent, there would be no need to collect it on delivery, which would save the postman from whom the letters were collected much needless work. A little later Hill had another brilliant idea; if every house-door had a narrow slit cut into it, the letters could easily be thrust into it and the postmen would not have to waste time waiting for someone to answer the door.

Next he had to decide how the postage could best be paid; he realised that to pay it in coin would mean more work when the letters were handed in. Then he made another constructive suggestion:

> Perhaps this difficulty might be obviated by using a bit of paper just large enough to bear the stamp, and covered at the back with a glutinous wash which, by applying a little moisture, might be attached to the letter.

To make this more convenient still, the letter, instead of being sealed, might be placed in 'one of the little bags called envelopes'.

Thus Rowland Hill suggested objects which seemed novel in his time though they are commonplace in our own: the letter-box, the postage-stamp and the envelope.

He forecast that his scheme would produce a large increase in the number of letters posted, so large, indeed, that a charge of a penny per ounce would not merely pay the cost of the postal service but give the Government a large profit.

Soon his pamphlet *Post Office Reform* was being read and discussed throughout the country. Naturally many people disagreed with all these 'new-fangled notions'. One writer declared that to use a stamp, or stamped cover, was 'universally admitted to be quite the reverse of convenient, and foreign to the habits of the people'; another foreboded gloomily that the penny post would make it easy to spread revolutionary ideas, and a noble lord asked indignantly if he were really expected to cut a hole in his mahogany door.

Others, however, realised the value of Rowland Hill's scheme and helped to make it well known. Henry Cole, for example, found ingenious ways of showing how absurd the older methods of fixing postal charges really were. He prepared two letters, one consisting of a large sheet of paper weighing one ounce, and the other of two tiny sheets weighing much less, displayed them in public and passed them round the House of Commons, pointing out that the small letter would be charged twice as much as the larger one. And he drew an amusing sketch of a mail-coach carrying six huge sacks of franked letters and so forth, which travelled free, and one small bag of ordinary letters marked 'pay £93'!

As knowledge of the scheme began to spread, numerous meetings were held in its favour. When a Member of Parliament handed in a petition praying for its adoption and the Speaker asked other Members who had similar petitions to bring them forward, many of them rose, cheering, to hand the petitions in.

In 1837, when King William IV died, the young Queen Victoria, who took her duties very seriously, was implored to help introduce Penny Postage, and one of the primary acts of her first Parliament was to appoint a Select Committee:

> ... to enquire into the present rates and mode of charging and collecting postage with a view to such reduction thereof as may be made without injury to the revenue; and for this purpose to examine especially into the mode recommended for charging and collecting postage in a pamphlet published by Mr Rowland Hill.

The Committee, whose Chairman was Robert Wallace, the man who had given Hill so much help, sat for sixty-three days during which time it examined over one hundred witnesses, including the Post Office authorities, many of whom were opposed to the new scheme. One of them declared that it would lead to so much letter-writing that the walls of the Post Office would burst, but Rowland Hill replied by inquiring whether the correspondence was meant to fit the building or the building to fit the correspondence!

During six days of questioning, he had not only to explain his scheme but to reply to the objections raised by the Post Office. Though annoyed by their opposition, he later realised that it was quite natural: introducing the new scheme would not merely cause them an immense amount of trouble, it would also suggest that they were slow-witted for not having devised something similar themselves. He knew what it

was to be pestered by eccentric people with weird ideas, and he realised that, from the point of view of the Post Office, he had simply been another crank whose ideas were more peculiar than usual.

After a careful inquiry, the Select Committee reported strongly in favour of postal reform and produced yet another Blue Book. Then the scheme had to go before Parliament. On 29th July 1839 the Bill introducing it was passed by the House of Commons, but it still had to go before the House of Lords, where the Duke of Wellington, whose opinion would sway many votes, was thought to be against such reform; indeed, he was against it, but he could see its qualities and at last he said, 'I shall, although with great reluctance, vote for the Bill, and I earnestly recommend you to do the same.' The Lords took his recommendation and so, on 17th August, the Royal assent was given, and penny postage became law.

Gaining public support for his scheme had imposed much hard work not only on Rowland Hill but on his wife Caroline, whom he had known since he was a boy, and who had given him considerable help;

35

when somebody called Hill 'the father of penny postage', one of his relatives replied: 'Then I know who was its mother!'

Much work still had to be done before the new system could be enforced, and most people expected that Rowland Hill, through whose efforts it had been adopted, would be put in charge of it, as he himself had hoped. Instead he was appointed for a period of two years to the Treasury, where he could keep an eye on its administration but where he would find it much more difficult to supervise.

No sooner was he appointed than he visited the Post Office to see how it was run, and in order to complete his own duties he rose every day at six and set off to the Treasury, to the surprise of its officials, who were accustomed to much shorter official hours; he also made a special visit to Paris to study the French postal system.

One of his tasks, which caused him much trouble and took a considerable amount of time, was to help choose a suitable design for the new postage stamps: he had many suggestions to consider, for the problem had been thrown open to public competition. It was indeed quite difficult; the stamps had to be produced cheaply but the design upon them very difficult to forge. It had to be easy to recognise, too, for otherwise people might have spurious stamps foisted on them.

Finally it was decided that there was only one nationally recognisable design – a portrait of the Queen. This, very carefully engraved so as to make forgery almost impossible, accordingly appeared on the first

two stamps ever issued, the famous 'penny black' and the 'twopenny blue'.

As these were the only postage-stamps then issued, there seemed no need to add the name of the country that had issued them. They set a tradition which has ever since been followed: whereas the postage stamps of other lands may bear almost any design and always show the name of their country, the words 'Great Britain' *never* appear on stamps, and whatever other designs they incorporate British stamps always bear a portrait of the reigning sovereign.

The new postal system was introduced in two stages. Early in December the postage rate was lowered to a penny for deliveries in London and fourpence for the rest of the country, odd charges like an extra penny to cross certain bridges and a halfpenny to cross the Scottish Border being removed; this gave the postal staff practice in handling large quantities of letters before the Penny Post came into force.

They certainly needed this practice for when Penny Postage was introduced on 10th January 1840, about 110,000 letters were posted, some being addressed by total strangers to the man who had introduced it. Crowds flocked to post their letters at the Central Post Office in St Martin's-le-Grand, and when the office closed for the day they gave three cheers, first for 'the penny postage and Rowland Hill', and then for the postal staff who had coped so manfully with the flood of letters.

Although the new system worked splendidly, the Post Office authorities still disliked it, and did their best to make Hill's work more difficult. When there came a change of Government, the new administration also disliked it and in July 1842 dismissed him; and when he offered to work for a time without any salary they refused.

This caused widespread indignation and Hill himself was greatly distressed. Not only had he got to find new employment at the age of forty-seven, but he feared that the Post Office would now ruin his work by increasing the postal charges. He was relieved, however, to find that the charges were not in fact to be increased; so although he could no longer play a part in running it, his system would still go on.

So well-known a man was unlikely to be out of employment long. Soon he was invited to join the Board of Directors of the London and Brighton Railway, which had been badly managed and become a muddle. Even one of its Directors who had protested, 'We want no Rowland Hills here to interfere in everything and perhaps even to introduce penny fares in all directions,' at last agreed that Hill could probably put things right.

So indeed he could; having reformed the Post Office, he reformed the railway, speeding up the ordinary trains, introducing expresses and Sunday excursions, and having branch lines built. Resulting from his work, the London, Brighton and South Coast Railway, as it was then called – it is now part of British Railways (Southern Region) – though small compared with some of the other lines, was equally efficient.

In 1846 came another change of Government. Almost at once, in response to public demand, Hill was appointed to the Post Office to complete the reforms which he had begun. Though he now had to give up his work as Director, not only of the L.B. & S.C.R. but of two other lines, which meant a serious reduction of his salary, he did not mind this, so intent was he on completing his life's work.

He visited several provincial towns, trying to improve the local services, and at Bristol the postal clerks and postmen thanked him for the help he had given them. He introduced more efficient methods of dealing with money orders, and arranged for the value of unclaimed orders to be used to provide life insurance for the postal staff. He further pleased them by releasing them from all Sunday work that was not absolutely necessary.

Following that, another problem occurred for him to solve; railways had replaced the old stage coaches, and letters were now being sorted on the trains, but what was to happen to letters for places near London, St Albans and Watford, for example, for the letters ought to be sorted before the trains reached these towns? Again he had a brilliant idea: such letters should be taken much further out and sorted on the down-train, and then returned to those towns on the up-train.

Rowland Hill had a hand in making many other improvements to the Postal Service. Naturally some people disliked these and attacked him through the post or in the papers; one man even threatened to kill him on his way to work, but Hill took no notice of the threat and, armed only with his umbrella, walked to the office in his ordinary way. In the 1860s he found it increasingly difficult to work with his chief and so, in 1864, at the age of sixty-eight, seriously ill, and worn out by over-work, Rowland Hill resigned.

After a long rest he was able to take an interest in public affairs once more, especially in the working of the Post Office; he also served on a Royal Commission on the Railways, and there too he gave splendid service. He was still a keen student of astronomy, and he wrote a long account of his life and duties in connection with the Post Office.

Fifteen years after his retirement his health failed. When he was honoured by being awarded the Freedom of the City of London, he was too ill to go to the Guildhall, as was the custom, to receive it; and when a deputation, headed by the City Remembrancer, bestowed the honour on him in his bedroom, he scarcely had the strength to sign the Register.

After his death, on 27th August 1879, he was buried in Westminster Abbey near the tomb of James Watt. Statues were erected to him not only in his birthplace, Kidderminster, but outside the Royal Exchange in London (it has since been transferred to its present site outside King Edward Building near St Paul's) and soon London street boys were adding their own memorial to him by sticking postage stamps on its pedestal.

Queen Victoria had knighted him in 1860, and he had become one of the best-known and most honoured men in the country. Letters were duly delivered to him, even though they were addressed only 'To him who gave us the Penny Post' to 'Rowland Hill – where he is' and even to 'Mr Owl O'Neill'!

He had given Britain a cheap and efficient postal service which was soon copied all over the world. He had encouraged trade and manufacture, and had greatly improved the conditions of the postal staff by whom the service he had introduced is carried out. He had done good work for Britain's railways, both as Director of three lines and by service on the Royal Commission. Moreover, thanks to his work, as one writer explained, 'The poor can at last write to one another just as if they were M.P.'s', an epitaph he would have valued more than the bust in Westminster Abbey and the statue near St Paul's.

Save the Children

LORD SHAFTESBURY
(1801–1885)

ALTHOUGH Robert Owen's schemes attained wide publicity the people whom he most influenced were the working-men; the mill-owners, other employers and ruling classes paid him little attention; for, after all, who was he? Apart from having rather fanciful schemes for communities, he was what is sometimes called a 'nobody', a self-educated man of the people, a former 'counter-jumper' who even lacked the sense to retain his money. When rank and gentility meant much more than they do today, such a person could have little influence. In order to really arouse public attention the requirement was a nobleman by birth, well known in society, with a public school and university education; someone who belonged to what is now called the 'Establishment'.

Anthony Ashley Cooper, born in London on 28th April 1801, was the eldest son of Lord Shaftesbury, who owned rich estates at St Giles, Dorset. His mother was descended from the Duke of Marlborough. His father was harsh and overbearing and ruled his family by fear, while his mother was cold-hearted and seemed to care little for her children. Little Anthony would, indeed, have been almost friendless were it not for an old servant of the family, Maria Millis, who gave him the affection he needed and brought some happiness into his life, and also gave him a sincere religious faith which he always retained.

He was even more unhappy when he went to school, and years later the memory made him shudder. 'Nothing could have surpassed it,' he wrote in his diary, 'for filth, bullying, neglect, and hard treatment of every sort.' When he was at home he cried at the idea of going to school, and when he was at school he cried at the thought of returning home. To complete his distress, Maria Millis died when he was about eight, but he never forgot her and always spoke of her as the best friend he had ever had.

He was happier when, at the age of twelve, he went to Harrow, but while walking down the Hill on one occasion he saw a scene which horrified him. Some drunken men lurched along the street carrying a burden and singing a vulgar song. When they fell over and dropped their burden he realised that it was a coffin: they were burying one of their workmates. Appalled at the sight, Anthony determined there and then, that he would devote his life to helping the down-trodden and oppressed.

Later he risked a severe punishment when he had to compose some Latin verse as was the custom, for instead of the usual dignified subjects he chose 'Duck-puddle, a mosquito-breeding pond' near the school. Had his masters thought that he was being impudent there would have been trouble, but they simply took the hint and the pond was filled in.

His father had meant him to become an officer, but military life did not appeal to Anthony who went instead to Oxford, where he got a first-class degree, and then travelled on the Continent, studied hard and read. He had decided to enter politics, but first came the problem: how could the ideals of Christianity be applied in such a career?

His hatred of cruelty was increased by the tragic death of his twelve-year-old brother, who, while at Eton, was killed in a sixty-round fight which lasted two hours. The fight had been so fierce that his opponent, who was two years older and a head taller than his victim, was accused of manslaughter but managed to escape punishment.

As the eldest son of an Earl, Anthony had his own title, Lord Ashley, and though this did not entitle him to a seat in the House of Lords it facilitated his entry into the House of Commons. In 1826 he was elected M.P. for Woodstock, and a year later he served on a Committee appointed to inquire into the treatment of lunatics; this, he found, was so harsh that almost until the end of his life he endeavoured, as Chairman of the Board of Commissioners in Lunacy, to improve conditions in the asylums. The two Bills he steered through Parliament have been called the 'Magna Carta of the Insane'.

Had he wished, he might have become a leading member of the Government and perhaps even Prime Minister, but he preferred to remain a private member and devote his life to trying to relieve the many hardships which the Industrial Revolution had produced. Though at times his reluctance to accept any honours rather distressed her, his wife, Lady Emily Cooper, whom he married in 1830, supported him loyally and brought him and their ten children the happiness he had lacked in his own childhood.

Soon came the chance for which Ashley had waited. Robert Owen was not the only person appalled at conditions in the factories, and many of the factory workers had protested and found educated men to lead them. They also needed someone to represent them in Parliament, and in 1829 they found him: Michael Sadleir, M.P. for Newark.

Sadleir lost no time, and in 1831 he introduced the Ten Hours Bill, aimed at shortening the children's working-day. Although his Bill was not passed, he was appointed Chairman of a Select Committee on Factory Children's Labour.

His Committee's report shocked the country. It showed that many of the children were not only over-worked and underpaid but savagely beaten; to tend the machines they had to crouch beneath them and twist awkwardly, with the result that they became permanently deformed and prematurely aged cripples. Even in the more humane factories, where their working-day was *only* twelve hours long, their health deteriorated considerably.

In the Elections of 1832 and 1834 Sadleir was defeated. A year later he died, only fifty-five years old but worn out by his efforts on behalf of the children, who were thus left with nobody to plead for them in Parliament.

His supporters had to find someone to replace him, and at last they decided to ask Lord Ashley, whose work on the Lunacy Commission had impressed them. After earnest thought, for he was never one to make rash decisions, and having consulted his wife, Ashley tried to re-introduce the Ten Hours Bill in 1833.

The workers were enraged when they found that the only result of his efforts was the appointment of another Commission to investigate the children's work, and they realised that the Commissioners who made the investigations seemed to be unsympathetic men whom they could not trust. The Commissioners' report did nothing to reassure them: it forbade the employment of children under nine and limited the working-day of those under thirteen; but it seemed to imply that it hardly mattered how long people above that age had to work.

The report aroused many protests in Parliament and out, and when the mill-owners complained that if the children's work was altered they would be ruined, it hardly convinced anyone. As the writer, William Cobbett, said bitterly, at one time Britain's trade and prosperity had been supposed to depend on her Royal Navy and her Merchant Service or the Bank of England. Now, it seemed, it depended on the toil of her little girls – if they worked two hours per day less the country

would be ruined! Ashley himself was so disappointed with the proposals that he washed his hands of them.

The result of the argument was the Factory Act of 1833, which in spite of serious faults did much for the children. In all mills – except, for some reason, silk mills – children under nine were not to be employed at all, and those under thirteen were not to be employed for more than forty-eight hours per week or nine in one day; and until they were eighteen young people were not to be employed for more than twelve hours a day or sixty-nine per week. Most important of all, the factories were to be properly inspected to ensure that these rules were kept.

None the less, the weaknesses of the Act resulted in little improvement for many of the children. Feeling that Ashley had failed them, the workers sought other leaders, but when they found that the Government intended to lengthen the working-day of children over eleven to twelve hours, they again asked him to become their leader. He first persuaded the Government not to lengthen the hours, as planned, and then he spent years collecting fresh evidence concerning factory conditions in order to prepare the way for a more satisfactory Act.

He had many difficulties to overcome, the mill-owners reminding him sarcastically that working conditions in the factories were little worse than those on the land and that on his own ancestral estates they were very bad indeed. He could not deny this, for his father, Lord Shaftesbury, who controlled the estates, had no sympathy whatever with his ideals and indeed the two had bitterly quarrelled about them. All that Ashley could do was to make up his mind that when he was estate-owner things should be very different.

The new Ten Hours Bill he introduced was making good progress when he thought it his duty to leave Parliament because he differed from the Government on another question. In spite of his absence the Bill became law, limiting the working-day not only for children and young people but also cutting down to twelve hours for women; and there was great rejoicing throughout the country.

Soon, however, it was clear that even this Act had its weak point. Many factories simply divided the ten hours working-day into two shifts, one early and one late. As there was not time for them to go home and rest between the shifts, many of the women and children had to stay in the factory for a twelve or thirteen hour day, so that they

45

were little better off than before.

Ashley, who had now re-entered Parliament, worked for another Act that while overcoming this weakness would grant something for which the factory workers were now clamouring, a ten hour day not only for women and children but for men. This proved far more difficult than he had expected, and against his will he was forced to agree to a ten-and-a-half hour working-day.

The workers were furious; they felt that they had been cheated and that he had failed them, so forgetting what he had done for them, they denounced him at a number of public meetings as a turncoat and a traitor. Hurt though he was by this, Ashley's conscience was clear, for he had done the best that he possibly could for them, and, however they felt about him, he would still go on working on their behalf.

Although it had disappointed them, the Factory Act of 1850 had done much for the men: it was the first time in Britain that their working-day had been limited at all, and it prepared the way for other Acts to shorten it still further. In 1874 the men were at last granted their ten hour day, and since then their conditions have been greatly improved. Long before this they realised that they had been grossly unjust to Ashley and saw how much they owed to his work.

His work had not been limited to the factories; he had long been concerned about conditions in the mines. In an eloquent speech in the House of Commons in 1840 he had declared, 'The hardest labour in the worst room in the worst conducted factory is less hard, less cruel, and less demoralising than the labour in the best of the coal-mines.' Though the Members may have felt that things could not be as bad as that, they appointed a Commission to inquire into the matter.

The Commission's report was even more shocking than that on the factories, for conditions in the mines were far worse than anyone could have supposed. Not only were women and young children employed underground, they were treated even more harshly than the men – and the treatment of the men was far from gentle. They had to toil in continual danger to life or limb, in an atmosphere sometimes laden with explosive or noisome gas, in dimly lit galleries so full of slime they were little better than sewers and with roofs so low that an ordinary-sized dog would have had to crouch. Some of the boys, lying on their backs, had to hack away at the coal above them in seams too thin to

accommodate a man.

Even more exacting was the toil of the 'hurriers'. In the larger galleries women, and in the smaller ones children, crawling on hands and knees and very scantily clad, were harnessed by chains to 'corves' loaded with coal and had to drag them along. If the corve simply slid, it might contain one or two hundredweight of coal, but if it had wheels, up to five hundredweight. With two children pulling it, the load might be nine hundredweight, and with one child pulling and two pushing with their heads – which wore away the hair, leaving bald spots – twelve hundredweight.

Girls had to carry up steep ladders baskets strapped to their backs and foreheads, and so piled up with coal that a grown man could not lift them without injuring himself. Other children had to work the pumps down in the pits for a twelve-hour day, standing in slimy water up to their ankles and sometimes up to their knees, and occasionally a child of three or four years old might be taken underground to hold a candle so that his father could work.

An easier task was that of the 'trappers' who had to open and close the doors which formed part of the mine's ventilating system as the loads of coal passed, yet they had to work almost in darkness with water dripping round them and rats stealing their food; and, the Commissioners declared, some were so frightened and lonely that they went mad.

Some children served as 'engine men' to work the hoisting machinery. This may sound exciting – but not when it had to be done day after day in all weathers, and when a moment's inattention might mean a serious accident. Three men were killed because the engine man turned away from his levers to look at a mouse; that engine man was nine years old.

The children were bullied and beaten to keep them at work, and by the end of the day's labour they were too tired to play, or possibly even to eat; all they wanted to do was to sleep. So frequent and disregarded were accidents that on seeing a funeral people might say, 'Oh, it's only a collier.' Many of those who were not killed in the mines developed industrial diseases and died, as one old miner said, 'Like rotten sheep.'

Realising that people might not want to wade through pages of print, the Commission had their Report illustrated with sketches made on the spot, of the women and children at work, which attracted attention and induced people to read it; the clear style in which it was written added to its effect.

Ashley took advantage of the horror aroused by the Report to introduce a Bill excluding all women and girls and all boys under thirteen from the mines. The Commons passed it with little alteration, but the House of Lords rejected it, for some of its most influential Members were mine-owners. They declared that the Report greatly exaggerated the hardships of work in the mines, and even said that the job of the 'trapper' who opened and closed the ventilating doors was quite pleasant!

But there was a force stronger than the House of Lords: public opinion. The whole nation was roused and was determined to put an end to this evil, the employment of women and children in the mines; and ended it was by the Mines Act of 1842.

There was another trade, Ashley declared, in which conditions were ten times worse than in the factories. Most chimneys were at that time cleaned by making small boys climb up them; if they objected the soles of their feet were prodded with wire, or straw was burned beneath them. Occasionally, when a chimney caught fire, the boy might be made to climb into it to extinguish the burning soot. Six was thought to be a 'nice trainable age' for the 'climbing boys'; below that they were more likely to be killed.

In worming their way through the narrow flues the 'climbing boys' were of course bruised and grazed and cut, so their masters hardened their skins by the painful process of rubbing them with the strongest brine. As one master-sweep explained:

> At first they will come back from their work with their arms and knees streaming with blood, and the knees looking as if the caps had been pulled off. Then they must be rubbed with brine again and perhaps go off to another chimney.

Some people, of course, had long sympathised with the sweeps and tried to help them, especially after 1785, when Jonas Hanway had written a book describing their sufferings; and Acts had been passed to protect them. On the other hand, most people felt that their sufferings had been exaggerated, and that it was impossible to sweep chimneys properly without them; and the Acts had seldom been enforced. Gadgets, like those used today, had been invented for chimney sweeping, but most housewives believed, and most master-sweeps pretended, that these would smother the furniture with soot.

Ashley spent years, in the intervals of his other work, trying to make the employment of climbing boys illegal, and after much difficulty he succeeded in having several Acts passed. These, too, were seldom enforced, and he saw that he would have to wait until public opinion was on his side; already such books as *The Water Babies* and *Oliver Twist* were arousing it.

In 1872 came his chance: a boy of seven had been sent up a flue and taken out dead fifteen minutes later. At once, in spite of his own distress, for his wife was then dying, Ashley made a public appeal in *The Times*. Another death followed, and then another: a boy died of exhaustion after going up a chimney and getting his lungs full of soot. Public opinion was at last aroused. In 1875 he sent an effective Bill through Parliament, and the work and sufferings of the climbing boys came to an end.

Ashley was distressed not only by the conditions in which people worked but by those in which they lived. After visiting the slums

49

several times – and coming out covered with vermin – he strove to make the nation realise the need in our great cities for proper housing, for sanitation, fresh air, clean water and unadulterated food. He pointed out that in London many buildings were overcrowded, several families sharing one room. Conditions in the common lodging-houses were even worse: in some five people shared the same bed, while in others there were no beds at all, the lodgers simply huddling together in filthy, verminous straw or rags scattered on the floor, yet the charges for such accommodation were unreasonably high.

Encouraged by the Prince Consort, he worked with the Society for Improving the Condition of the Working Classes to set up 'model lodging houses'. These were clean and free from vermin or overcrowding, and their charges were low, yet they managed to pay their way. The bill he promoted for the Registration and Inspection of Common Lodging Houses was said by Charles Dickens to be the best ever passed by an English Parliament.

This work led him to realise the havoc that lack of cleanliness and sanitation was producing in the Crimean War and he helped send out a Sanitary Commission to investigate it. Florence Nightingale declared that the success of her work in the Crimean hospitals owed more to him than anyone else, and that his Commission had 'saved the British Army'.

Ashley had long been greatly distressed by the plight of the waifs and strays, the neglected children of the slums. He was seeking some method of befriending them, when he chanced to see an appeal in *The Times* for help in running a 'Ragged School' near Holborn. The Ragged Schools Union had been formed to carry on the work started many years earlier by John Pounds, a crippled shoemaker of Portsmouth. Not content with trying to educate them, the Union also befriended the uneducated and friendless children. Its work was greatly helped when Ashley became their President, for his reputation made the schools better known and led other people to assist them.

When a city missionary told him that 'forty thieves' were hoping that he might help them to become honest, he spent a whole evening discussing the problems of about four hundred men, all of whom had been in jail and some of whom were criminals. He promised to do his best and indeed helped about three hundred of them to find honest

work at home or overseas.

His great aim, however, was not so much to enable ex-criminals to reform as to prevent people from becoming criminals. One of the greatest causes of crime and poverty, he realised, was drink; but he also realised that it was not the only cause, and that poverty might drive people to drink. So, without being a rigid teetotaller or pro-hibitionist, Ashley tried to find ways of reducing the evils of excessive drinking. He tried to make it illegal for wages to be paid in public-houses, and he urged the working-men to stay out of them.

Although, to avoid confusion, we have continued to call him Ashley, he had become the Seventh Earl of Shaftesbury. His father, the Sixth Earl, had died in 1851, and he had succeeded both to the family name and to the family estates.

The new Lord Shaftesbury soon realised how well justified were the accusations made against conditions on his estates: some of the cottages he owned were overcrowded, filthy, and unhealthy; but what was he to do? His work had been very expensive and had kept him too busy to earn money, of which he was now in desperate need. 'Why, there are things here to make one's flesh creep,' he wrote in his diary, 'and I have not a farthing to set them right.'

Yet he could not bear to do nothing. Although it distressed him to part with property which had been in the family for many years, it hurt him still more to see people suffer. By selling some valuable paintings and part of his land he was enabled to build cottages and schools, to raise his people's wages, to create employment by starting large drainage schemes, and to make their lives more pleasant by organising cricket clubs and evening schools and awarding prizes for allotments.

His attempts to improve his estates showed him that children working on the land were almost as badly treated as those in the factories and mines: they too were overworked, poorly paid and harshly punished. Gangs of children, six years old and upwards, were set to work, sometimes miles away from their homes, on such tasks as planting and picking potatoes, weeding and spreading manure, their backs aching because of the continual stooping and their fingers bruised, blistered and bleeding.

He pleaded for these children in the House of Lords, and six years later, in 1873, some of the reforms for which he had worked were accomplished. No longer, for example, could children of under ten be employed on the land.

His life-long devotion to his work gave him little leisure for rest or recreation, and he found it difficult to make friends. Distress at the sufferings he saw around him so filled his mind that he could think of little else.

Such work as his was bound to make him enemies and to make him liable to attack at public meetings and in the Press. One attack, made in an American paper when he denounced negro slavery, went far astray:

> Who is this Lord Shaftesbury? Some unknown lordling . . . It is a pity he does not look at home! Where was he when Lord Ashley was fighting for the Factory Bill and pleading the cause of the English slave? We never even heard the name of Lord Shaftesbury then!

No wonder, for Lord Shaftesbury was Lord Ashley at the time!

Anthony Ashley Cooper, Seventh Earl of Shaftesbury, died on 1st October 1885. As he wished, he was buried not in Westminster Abbey but in the church near his home at St Giles, Dorsetshire. A Memorial Service was, however, held in the Abbey and it was attended by members not only of the Royal Family and the nobility and Parliament but of the ordinary people for whom he had done so much: miners, factory girls, children from the Ragged Schools, men who had once been climbing boys. And outside, in spite of the bad weather, the streets were crowded with mourners of every class.

His statue in the Abbey bears his name – but how many of those who see the Eros Statue in Piccadilly Circus remember that it, too, is a memorial to Lord Shaftesbury? Still, years after his death, the splendid schools and homes run by the Shaftesbury Society not merely commemorate his name but continue his work. Yet his greatest achievement is 'conspicuous by its absence' – the absence of climbing boys from our chimneys and children from our factories, and of women and children from our mines.

E

Awards for Eminence

ALFRED BERNHARD NOBEL
(1833–1896)

EXPLOSIVES are useful in peace as well as in war; they are used by canal-excavators and road-builders, miners and railway engineers, wherever hard rocks have to be blasted away. Although gunpowder has long been known, it is not really powerful enough, and many inventors have tried, sometimes at the risk of their lives, to produce something more efficient.

A few of them even trained their sons to continue their work, and it was into one of these inventive families that Alfred Bernhard Nobel was born, in Stockholm on 21st October 1833. Indeed, one of his earliest memories – he was only four at the time – was of being scared on hearing an explosion in the backyard shed where his father Immanuel worked, and of seeing the neighbours crowding round with angry gestures and words. So alarmed were the authorities that they forbade such experiments anywhere in the city.

Immanuel had begun his tests because he believed that a new explosive would help in cutting the Suez Canal which was then being planned, but he realised that it would be equally useful in war, and he thought that the Russian army would welcome it. In 1837 he emigrated to St Petersburg, and five years later invited his family to join him; he had designed a number of land-mines that exploded if trodden on, as well as sea-mines that exploded at the touch of a ship.

Alfred, who was then nine years old, may not have felt very pleased for, like Louis Braille and Rowland Hill, he had been a weakly infant; his childhood was unhappy, as was that of Lord Shaftesbury. It was not that his parents neglected or ill-treated him and though he was a little scared of his father he was devoted to his mother Caroline Andrietta, but he was one of those unfortunate people who are melancholy by nature all their lives.

When he arrived in Russia he was still weak and so he remained until he was about fifteen, when he suddenly shot up and grew very tall. He was brilliant at his studies, learning English and several other languages quite easily and reading widely, but he was still unhappy; when his father sent him to America he was not excited, as most people are, but only bored by his first sight of the sea, and when he visited the supposedly 'gay city', Paris, it did not cheer him up at all.

Returning to Russia in 1852, he joined his father's firm. They needed him badly, to help prepare for the Crimean War which broke out two years later; the Nobel factories were busy day and night on munitions, making not only mines and torpedoes but marine engines to convert the Russian Navy's 'wooden walls' into steamships. They had many difficulties to contend with, for most of their workmen were completely untrained and they were short of equipment: before they could build the engines they had to construct machine-tools, and before they could construct the tools they had to make hammers. The work was so hard that Alfred's health again broke down, and he was ordered to take a holiday.

Soon after his return to work the Crimean War ended and there was no longer a demand for munitions. The Nobels, whose factories had closed down, were almost ruined and the two parents returned to Sweden, where Alfred rejoined them in 1862.

Immanuel Nobel had not been discouraged, for he had had another scheme to make use of a new explosive, nitro-glycerine, which was uncertain and dangerous; its inventor, the Italian chemist Sobrero, who had been badly injured when a drop of it exploded and who found that its smell gave him violent headaches, had in desperation given up experimenting with it. Immanuel thought that if it were mixed with gunpowder it might make an excellent blasting-powder and he wanted his sons to work on these lines.

His sons did not at first welcome the idea. They were rather sceptical of their father's brain-waves – one of his ideas had been to propel torpedoes by harnessing them to trained seals! – and they knew that all previous attempts to use nitro-glycerine had failed. Nevertheless, the old man was so very insistent that Alfred thought he should try, and he was greatly annoyed to find, after the failure of one of his first experiments, that his father and one of his brothers were laughing at him.

By this time, however, he had become so seriously interested in the scheme that he continued his experiments. He found that when he put the gunpowder inside a glass tube and placed it inside a container of nitro-glycerine, it would explode under water but not on land. He decided that this reaction had occurred because the water had compressed the gunpowder for when he closed both ends of the glass tube with sealing-wax, his home-made bombs exploded both under water and on land.

He improved them by using the gunpowder as a detonator, its explosion serving to touch off the nitro-glycerine; then he substituted a more sensitive explosive, fulminate of mercury, for the gunpowder; it forms the well-known percussion cap. It worked so admirably that he patented this method of exploding nitro-glycerine and set up a laboratory for its manufacture. This led to a violent dispute with his father Immanuel, who thought that much of the credit was really due to himself.

Then came a disaster which made them forget their quarrel. In September 1864, Alfred's laboratory was destroyed in an explosion. One of the five men killed was his youngest brother Oscar; his job had been to keep the explosive cool, and it seemed probable that he had forgotten to watch the thermometer.

As before, the townspeople were thoroughly alarmed, and Alfred Nobel was forbidden to make explosives anywhere in Stockholm. But he was determined to go on manufacturing them, for now nitro-glycerine was being widely used; moreover, he had to make them within easy reach of a railway. He overcame the difficulty by building a new laboratory floating on the lake. He had to move it several times because the people on the shore got scared, but at last he towed it to the middle of the lake and worked there until he was able to build larger factories elsewhere on dry land.

Many people who handled nitro-glycerine did not realise how dangerous it could be, or were unable to recognise this oily-looking liquid. When some of it dripped out of a container on to the wheels of the cart that was carrying it, the driver was pleased for he thought that it was lubricating oil, and a woodcutter used a bottle of it for greasing his boots!

Those men were lucky, but others who handled nitro-glycerine were not. There were so many serious explosions, in which so much damage was done to property and so many lives lost that it was considered too dangerous to use, and some workers refused to have anything to do with it. People who wanted to sell or use it overcame this difficulty by simply calling it 'glonoin oil'.

Such a trick could never satisfy Nobel, and although he claimed that when properly handled the explosive was reasonably safe he determined to make it foolproof. Realising that a solid explosive would be less dangerous than a liquid which could be spilled, he tried to solidif nitro-glycerine by soaking various kinds of powder into it.

He indignantly denied the rumour that he had found the right type of powder by accident when a tin of nitro-glycerine had leaked into the packing around it; he had, he declared, discovered it as a result of systematic research. He had tried powdered charcoal, sawdust, brickdust and cement, none of which was satisfactory, for the result was either lumpy or pasty; sometimes the fault was that it had not absorbed enough of the liquid or simply that it would not explode. Then he experimented with a sort of clay so plentiful in Northern Germany that it was of hardly any value: it was kieselguhr, formed of tiny fossils called diatoms.

This produced a solid explosive as powerful as nitro-glycerine itself and far safer to handle. After further experiments to make certain that it was suitable for use, he sold his new explosive under two names, one showing its freedom from danger and the other (from the Greek word for power) its strength: what was once also called 'Nobel's Safety Powder' is now famous as 'Dynamite'.

The new explosive formed a terrible weapon in war. At the end of the Franco-Prussian War of 1870 the Germans used it to bombard

Paris with the first high explosive shells. It was equally terrible, when fanatical political extremists, the 'Dynamitards', used it in home-made bombs.

Nevertheless its value to peaceful law-abiding citizens outweighed its terrors; for mining, quarrying and civil engineering, wherever rock had to be blasted away, it soon became invaluable. As powerful as nitro-glycerine, it was far safer when used, transported or stored, quite safe indeed, if handled with reasonable care; far more powerful than gunpowder, it had the additional advantage of directing most of its blast not upwards, as gunpowder did, but downwards.

The British Government, which had banned nitro-glycerine for being too dangerous to use, gave permission for dynamite to be manufactured in Britain. It had to be made in the open country, of course, and Nobel heartily disliked the site of his factory at Ardeer, in Stirlingshire. As he wrote to a friend:

> If I hadn't got my work here, Ardeer would be the most depressing place in the world. Imagine everlasting bleak dunes with no buildings. Only the rabbits can find food here, and they eat something which is quite unjustifiably called grass, and of which you find only a few traces here and there. This is simply a desert, where the wind blows and howls, filling the ears with sand which drifts into the rooms like a fine drizzle. A few yards away the ocean begins and between us and America there is nothing but water.

But although he did not like it, he knew that this lonely place in the midst of the dunes was ideal for his work, and he took care that the 'greatest dynamite factory in the world' should put safety first. The explosive was manufactured in a number of small buildings, wide apart and separated by blast-proof banks of earth. Since production began in 1873, the factory has never suffered a serious accident, and later factories have been designed on much the same lines.

The sale of his explosives had made Nobel rich and famous, and he felt it his duty to meet other notable people by entering society. He had got over his dislike of Paris, and he realised that it was an excellent centre for a business-man with interests almost all over the world. He bought a large mansion near the Arc de Triomphe and furnished it by the simple plan of allowing an experienced interior-decorator to develop his own ideas, but he chose pictures personally, and instead of

buying them outright he hired them so that he could exchange them for others whenever he felt so inclined.

However, he could entrust the preparations of his work to nobody but himself. Small though his laboratory was, its equipment was specially chosen, and he appointed a competent assistant to supervise it. His study contained two desks, a large one for himself and a smaller one for his secretary – when he had a secretary, that is, for he never seemed to find anybody who satisfied him for long. The walls of both rooms were lined with books in several different languages; scientific works in the laboratory and volumes on history, literature, religion and so forth, in his study.

Although personally he disliked such events, he often gave banquets and arranged social evenings; and like many other men who are naturally unhappy he could be very good company when he wished and could make sure that his guests enjoyed themselves, although afterwards he might feel that he had been wasting his time. These events enabled him to meet influential people – V.I.P.s they would be called nowadays – such as one of his heroes, Ferdinand de Lesseps, who had successfully supervised the cutting of the Suez Canal and was planning another to cut the Isthmus of Panama.*

Although Nobel was interested in the Panama Canal scheme there was another project in which he was directly concerned. In 1873 his oldest brother Robert had gone to Baku on the Caspian Sea, with the idea of developing its immense oil-fields.

These had long been known; for as it oozed through clefts in the rocks, the oil easily caught fire, producing a strange landscape of flickering flames and billowing smoke in which the very earth appeared to be alight; it had long been a centre of pilgrimage, and on a headland there had, until recently, stood a Parsee fire-worshippers' shrine. When in the nineteenth century the Russians had taken over the region from Persia, the Czar had sent chemists to investigate its possibilities, but they had reported that this 'stinking black mass' was useless. In those days, too, mineral oils were for the most part used only as a basis for patent medicines – until the oil-lamp was invented, bringing a world-wide demand for paraffin.

Then the Baku oil-fields had been developed, but the methods used

* See *Engineers of the World*, pp. 109–119

were not very efficient. The 'stinking black mass' was baled from shallow pits by hand and carried in expensive barrels to a place six miles away, appropriately called Blacktown. Because it made such a mess, the charges made for shipping it across the Caspian were so very high that by the time it reached the Russian towns it cost more than oil shipped across the Atlantic from America.

Robert Nobel, who had already had experience in refining crude oil, realised that, though mechanising would be rather expensive, by using modern equipment the Baku oil-fields could be made to pay. After obtaining good results from an experimental refinery, he invited his two brothers, Ludwig and Alfred, to visit Baku with a view to drilling for oil on a really large scale.

Alfred refused, explaining that though he would like to be with his brothers, a 'waterless dusty oil-stained wilderness' had no attraction for him, but when Ludwig, after visiting Baku, assured him that a high-quality oil could be refined very easily, he agreed to help finance it. The three formed the Nobel Brothers' Naphtha Company, and soon oil-production was in full swing.

Alfred not only invested large sums of money in the company but suggested improvements in its working, such as a pipe-line between the harbour and the wells and a more efficient method of refining the oil, to make use of its former waste products.

Within a few years Baku became a large port with a refinery occupying a square mile of land and immense storage tanks each holding 4,000,000 gallons of oil. The Company owned over a thousand oil trucks on the railways and a fleet of the first tankers ever built, twenty large ones on the Caspian Sea and twelve small ones on the Volga. Robert was manager in Baku, Ludwig directed from his office in St Petersburg, and Alfred helped from Paris with money and ideas.

To house its thousands of workers, the Company built a special suburb, the soil for its park being shipped across the Caspian and its trees down the Volga. It provided married quarters, with dormitories for the unmarried workers, and with schools; its welfare services were far in advance of those of Britain, and Robert Owen and Lord Shaftesbury would certainly have approved of them.

Perhaps it was only by accident that Alfred Nobel had become a manufacturer of munitions; had his father, Immanuel, not interested

him in this work, he might have devoted his life to other branches of industry. Among his inventions were improved methods of manufacturing sulphuric acid, of purifying iron, and of constructing gas burners. Less successful was his scheme for rending the rocks without using explosives: by boring a hole in them and directing a sort of flame-thrower into it, then when water was poured over the heated rock it was made brittle and easy to excavate.

At times he admitted that the improvements in artillery, including war-rockets, on which he was working were 'rather fiendish', but he was so fascinated by the difficult problems they involved that he continued to work on them. In 1887 he first tried, as did several other chemists, to devise a smokeless powder and he succeeded by the simple method of combining two explosives, nitro-glycerine and nitro-cellulose (guncotton) with a little camphor. This ballistite, as he called it, was even more successful than he had expected.

Two of the British scientists who had also been working on this project had meanwhile produced another smokeless powder. Although they had discussed this problem with Nobel, they declared that they had invented cordite independently of him, while *he* claimed that they had been infringing his patents. When he took action against them, his claim was rejected, as it was when he appealed to the House of Lords.

This verdict, which he felt was quite unjust, embittered him. It was not only the money-loss that he suffered but his feeling of having been defrauded of his rights and that the British Government, whose sense of justice he had trusted, was bolstering up the fraud.

He had suffered other disillusions, too. Some of his trusted associates had betrayed him, and some of the many people whom he had generously assisted had proved unworthy of his help. The Panama Canal scheme, which had interested him so much, had been a fiasco: de Lesseps, though quite honest, had proved utterly incompetent, and other members of his company had deliberately perpetrated a fraud on the public.*

Then in 1888 he was dealt a severe blow. His brother Ludwig had died and some of the newspapers had mistakenly announced that he himself – Alfred Nobel – was dead, and in the obituaries had described him – Alfred – as the 'Dynamite King', a 'merchant of death'.

So that was how the world thought of him! That was how completely he had been misunderstood! At one time he had thought that if only explosives and other weapons could be terrible enough people would be afraid to fight, for they would realise that in modern warfare all the contestants would be devastated. So, if only for their own benefit, the rulers would try to settle their quarrels peacefully.

When he had had some experience of 'war hysteria', however, of mobs so infuriated that they were demanding war regardless of consequences, he realised that he had been wrong. Such people would be willing to risk their own country's devastation provided that the enemy's devastation was worse.

Although a friend tried to interest him in schemes for producing world peace by universal disarmament he did not think very highly of them; and even though he was impressed by the great men who were present when he attended an International Peace Congress held at Berne in 1892, he thought that the methods which they suggested were absurd. One of his own ideas was to try to regulate war much in the same way as duelling used to be regulated, but by international agreement; another was to try to persuade the governments to agree not to wage war for a year; they could hardly object to so short a delay, and

* See *Engineers of the World*, pp. 119-125

at the end of the year they might agree to another year's delay and so on: in that way peace might come with hardly anyone's realisation.

As peace was not likely to be made yet, he went on making munitions at his new factory in Bofors, Sweden; he had plans for improved war-rockets, which of course could also be used for peaceful purposes such as carrying rescue equipment to vessels shipwrecked off the coast. Another of his schemes was to take photographs from the air by attaching a camera, with an automatic shutter-release, to a parachute dropped from a balloon or rocket (aeroplanes had not yet been invented.)

He was enthusiastic for another project. A Swedish engineer, the experienced aeronaut Andrée, wished to attempt to soar over the North Pole in a balloon, taking photographs and making careful records during his flight. At first his scheme was ridiculed, but the help and publicity given to him by Nobel enabled him to set out in July 1897.*

Because his failing health demanded a warmer climate, Nobel bought an estate at San Remo, Italy; though he called it 'Mio Nido' ('My Nest') it was soon known as the 'Villa Nobel'. Its garden was large enough for him to fire guns and rockets out to sea, and a long iron pier enabled him to check their performance. It was large enough, too, to accommodate his well-equipped laboratory and his library.

He had plenty of other projects to work on, although experiments on guns and rockets still fascinated him, and he helped younger inventors, one of whom designed the first bicycle with a variable gear. He also wanted to adapt, for peaceful purposes, the chemicals used in making explosives; he attempted, for example, to produce artificial rubber and leather and silk from nitro-cellulose.

As his health deteriorated, he was sardonically amused at the failure of his doctors to diagnose his illness: one said that it was rheumatic gout and another that it was gouty rheumatism! He was amused, too, by the medicine prescribed for him – to avoid frightening their patients the doctors called it 'trinktin', but he knew that it was really nitro-glycerine!

---

* Andrée did not return from his flight, and not until 1930 was it known what had become of him. His balloon had come down only seven degrees from the Pole, and he and his two companions had died while trying to return on foot across the ice, still keeping up their records to the last.

In August 1896 his brother Robert died, and Alfred Nobel, who realised that his own end could not be far off, felt his loss keenly. He was still concerned about world peace, and a few weeks before his death he wrote to a friend to say that the peace movement was gaining ground, and that this was due to the civilisation of the ordinary people, especially to those who fought prejudice and ignorance; among these, he added, his friend held exalted rank.

Soon after he died, on 10th December 1896, his will showed that he too held exalted rank among those who fought prejudice and ignorance. Apart from a few small personal legacies, he had left his vast fortune to a special fund: it was to be invested, and its interest was to be given every year to those persons who during the previous year had rendered the greatest service to mankind.

There are five Nobel prizes: one each for the greatest discovery or invention in physics and in chemistry; one for the greatest discovery in physiology or medicine; one for the most outstanding work in literature 'of an idealistic tendency' – all awarded by some of Sweden's 'learned societies'. The fifth, awarded by a committee elected by the Norwegian Storthing (Parliament) is for the greatest effort to promote world peace by work for the brotherhood of nations, for abolishing or reducing the world's armaments, or for forming or helping to increase the influence of peace congresses.

The strange will aroused some argument, some Swedes feeling, for example, that Nobel had been unpatriotic in leaving the peace prize to be awarded by a foreign country with whom Sweden was not on the best of terms. His family were, naturally enough, not best pleased to find that they were to receive very little of his wealth, but they did not contest the will, for, like almost everybody else, they realised how splendid were its aims. The people chosen to award the prizes have always taken their work very seriously, and, quite apart from the monetary reward it brings, to receive a Nobel Prize is one of the greatest honours a thinker can be paid; it shows that the value of his work is recognised by the world.

Most of the scientific awards are made for achievements too technical to explain, but we can all understand why the first Nobel Prize for physics was given, in 1901, to Röntgen, for the discovery of X-rays, and why later prizes were awarded to the Curies; Einstein was, of course, another Nobel Prize-winner, and we can understand, too, how Fleming merited the award for medicine, made for his discovery of penicillin.

As the Nobel Prizes are open to all the world, those for literature are awarded whatever the language used. Seven have been given to British writers, including Rudyard Kipling, famous for his stirring poems and his short stories; G. B. Shaw, whose plays are very amusing, though they deal with serious subjects; and Winston Churchill, orator and historian.

Half of the first Peace Prize was awarded to Dunant, for his work in founding the Red Cross, and Nansen, the explorer, received the 1922 prize for the help he gave to the stateless 'displaced persons' of the First World War. Others have been awarded not to individuals but to societies which did much for world peace.

Nobel's explosives, once thought so dreadful, have been outstripped by others far more terrible, and though these have not, as he once hoped, made war impossible, rulers have become much more reluctant to wage it.

Yet his work lives on. No longer is Alfred Bernard Nobel known as a 'merchant of death', as the 'Dynamite King'. Nowadays his name is usually mentioned in connection with his prizes for eminence in science or literature, and especially with the Nobel Prize awarded for efforts to promote world peace.

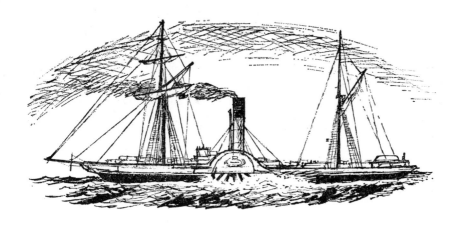

Safety at Sea

SAMUEL PLIMSOLL
(1824–1898)

BRITISH prosperity has long depended upon overseas trade, and since the nineteenth century the British have relied upon it not only to export the goods their machinery produces but to import their food. Yet for a long time conditions in their Merchant Service were worse even than those in their factories and mines; they endangered not only the seamen's well-being but their lives and the safety of their ships.

Born on 10th February 1824 in Bristol, Samuel Plimsoll spent most of his boyhood in Penrith, Cumberland. Little is known about his early life, except that he had several brothers and sisters, that he was educated first in a 'dame's school' and then by the curate as was usual in those days, and that he enjoyed hiking up Penrith Beacon to gaze at the glorious scenery of the Lake District. When he was fourteen, however, he had to leave Lakeland, for his father, as Excise officer, was transferred to Sheffield.

After a short period at school, Samuel became office-boy to a solicitor at a wage of only 3s. 6d. a week. Small though this pay was, he contrived to save a few shillings, and spent them on buying hare-skins which he could send to London to be sold at a profit. He was ambitious in other ways, too, and attended evening-classes to fit himself for something better than an office-boy's job.

He then became a clerk in a brewery firm, his wages beginning at a pound per week. He needed this higher pay, for his father had died and when only twenty Samuel had to support his widowed mother and her younger children. He was on good terms with his new employer and acted almost as his private secretary, writing speeches for him when he became Mayor of Sheffield.

He also made himself known in public life, serving as Honorary Secretary to an Exhibition held in Sheffield and rendering good service on the Relief Committees formed when accidents occurred in the coal-mines. This gained him so high a reputation that he was taken seriously when he proposed a method of increasing the coal trade by rail to London.

Unfortunately the railway rejected his scheme, and Plimsoll nearly ruined himself in trying to persuade them to adopt it. He had to buy a season ticket to London, and this was so expensive that for a time he had to lead a strange sort of 'double life'. When he was in Sheffield meeting influential people he had to keep up appearances, but during his visits to London he had to live in one of the 'model lodging-houses' which Lord Shaftesbury had helped to introduce. The rent was only three shillings a week, but at one time it left him with little more than eightpence a day for food!

He thought highly of the lodging-houses, but he thought even more highly of the men who lived in them. Poor though they were, if they had food or tobacco they were always ready to share it with those who had none. They gave him an admiration and sympathy for the 'working class' which he never lost.

At last he found employment with a firm of Sheffield colliery owners, and again he got on very well with his employers. They readily helped him in his negotiations with the railway company and quite approved when in 1857 he married Eliza Ann Railton, who was related to two influential members of the firm.

By this time he had become a London coal-merchant, the railway which had once refused to consider his scheme supplying him with fuel. Then he had a brilliant idea. Hitherto coal had been loaded and unloaded so carelessly that some of the lumps were ground into unsalable coal-dust. Plimsoll patented coal-shoots floored with iron bars,

slightly separated from one another, down which the coal slid. The dust fell through the gaps between the bars and the 'clean' coal slid down into the sacks, waggons or trucks.

This method of screening the coal paid him so well that he was able to build coal-drops, construct sidings and hire wharves where the coal could be loaded and unloaded and put into sacks. He prospered and did much to organise London's fuel supply; but that, though in itself a creditable achievement, was only the prelude to his life's work.

Now that he was a wealthy man he thought it his duty to enter politics. Having been defeated when he first stood for Parliament, in 1868 he was elected M.P. for Derby with a majority of over 2,000. For a time he was content to be an undistinguished member of the Liberal Party, until in 1870 he found a cause which demanded his enthusiastic support.

A Tynemouth shipowner, James Hall, was greatly distressed by the loss of life at sea, often caused by the unseaworthy condition of many of the ships. He drew public attention to it by writing to the *Shipping World* and *The Times*, and when in 1869 a Bill to regulate shipping was introduced in Parliament he was one of the experts who were asked to report on it.

He realised that the Bill was not strong enough. No ships, he urged, should be allowed to leave harbour unless they were seaworthy, and were approved by the underwriters (the firms that insure ships and pay compensation when they are damaged or lost). He also declared that they should be inspected periodically. If there were any doubt about their condition an inquiry should be held to decide whether or not they were seaworthy. Moreover, all vessels should have their hulls plainly marked with a load-line, and it should be an offence for them to carry so much cargo that this line was submerged. He explained these ideas in an eloquent speech at a meeting of the Associated Chambers of Commerce in London, and prepared a petition to be sent to Parliament.

Plimsoll, who was present at that meeting, was deeply impressed by the speech. As soon as he could escape from his Parliamentary duties he went specially to Newcastle to discuss these proposals with James Hall, who at once realised how useful it would be to have someone in Parliament to speak for the imperilled seamen.

As an M.P. Plimsoll could do more than speak for the seaman: he could demand information on shipping from the Board of Trade and seek further information from Lloyd's, that great association of underwriters which for so many years has done so much for British shipping, and he could interest other Members in safety at sea. As a wealthy man, he could travel to the seaports to consult the ship's officers, the port officials and the seamen. Moreover, being an educated man and a 'gentleman', he could talk to the officers and officials on equal terms, while his experience in the Shaftesbury lodging-houses had taught him how to understand the seamen.

Although he himself was a landsman and knew next to nothing about ships and the sea, he was determined to find out; he was appalled at the risks the seamen had to take as a result of the gross carelessness or dishonesty of some – but by no means all – of the owners and shipbuilders. He was distressed, too, that so many public-spirited people seemed to care so little about this situation. Here was a cause to which, with the full approval and ready help of his wife Eliza, he would devote most of his life.

The more he learned about the laws which regulated shipping the more he was amazed and angered: compiled as they had been piece-meal, some were unreasonable and a few seemed crazy. Laws meant to ensure the safety of houses were usually enforced, but those meant to ensure the safety of shipping were often ignored, and some were so badly worded that they could hardly be enforced at all. There were Acts of Parliament to regulate conditions in the factories and mines where landsmen worked, and in the lodging-houses where they lived, but few to regulate conditions on the vessels where seamen lived and worked.

If a factory-hand or a miner thought his work too unpleasant or dangerous he could leave, but if a seaman who had 'signed on' were to leave his ship, he would be imprisoned, even though conditions on board might be intolerable or the ship seemed likely to sink as soon as she left port.

True, he would escape punishment if he could *prove* that his vessel was dangerously undermanned or unseaworthy – though it was not enough to prove that she was dangerously overloaded. But how could he prove it? He was often not allowed to give evidence before the magistrate, and if the magistrate were to decide that the complaint was unjustified the seaman who had made it had to pay for the costs of the inquiry out of his wages.

In the days when National Insurance was unheard of, shipowners were not compelled to compensate any sailor who was injured or crippled for life on one of their vessels, nor to compensate the widow of a sailor who went down with the ship. A seaman might sign on before he saw the vessel upon which he was to sail – this was sometimes hard to avoid – but if as soon as he saw her he realised that she was one of the 'coffin ships', as they were called, never likely to reach their destination, then he had a dreadful choice to make. If he jumped ship he risked going to prison and leaving his wife and children penniless, but if he stayed on board he risked death and leaving his wife a widow and his children fatherless.

James Hall had given examples of the tragedies caused by unsea-worthy or grossly overloaded vessels. Old ships, though fit only for scrap, might be bought very cheaply by unscrupulous owners and then sent to sea again, perhaps insured far above their value: and if they foundered it was purely luck if there were no loss of life. One such vessel,

nearly thirty years old, had sailed though her rigging was defective and she was taking in more water than her pumps could cope with; after three days at sea captain and crew had abandoned ship. Other vessels had been overloaded until their decks were awash; one of these had gone down with all hands.

Plimsoll succeeded in making Parliament aware of such evils, and the Government was anxious to abolish them. They had already passed the Bill on which Hall had been asked to report, and they had prepared another Bill empowering the Board of Trade to stop and inspect any vessel which seemed unfit to put to sea. Moreover, Plimsoll himself had induced Parliament to appoint a Royal Commission on Unseaworthy Ships. But he was still dissatisfied, especially as little improvement seemed likely for the sailors or their dependants; though passengers or their next of kin could be compensated for injury or death at sea the seamen or their widows could not.

He realised that if any action were to be taken it could not be left to Parliament. An appeal to public opinion was needed; the conscience of the nation must be aroused.

Choosing a period when Parliament was not sitting, he went to a small fishing-village where he could work undisturbed, and wrote his appeal to the nation. Appearing early in 1873, it bore a title which, though simple, was likely to awaken interest: *Our Seamen*.

By modern standards it was not very well written. Descriptions of shipwrecks and of the sailors' hardships and perils were strangely mingled with appeals to the readers and – for Plimsoll was a religious man – with prayers and Bible texts. This, however, surprised the people of the time less than it would ourselves, and it helped to impress readers with his sincerity. Still more impressive were the illustrations: drawings of badly overloaded ships, and photographs of widows and orphans which awakened the sympathy of people who otherwise might never have been stirred.

The great fault was that in his anxiety to help the seamen Plimsoll had been far too ready to rush into print. He had angered James Hall by including information that had been given him in confidence and when he was rebuked for this his apology had been very half-hearted. Not realising that sailors are not always truthful, especially when they have a grudge against the shipowners, and that even truthful sailors may exaggerate or be mistaken, he made accusations without first troubling to ensure that they were well founded.

He accused some shipowners of being wantonly careless of their sailors' lives and others of sending unseaworthy vessels to sea, hoping to receive the insurance money if the ships were wrecked, and although he did not mention any names he implied whom he meant. It is not surprising, therefore – though it seems to have surprised him – that he was threatened with actions for libel and that ship-owning M.P.s who felt that he had libelled them should also protest in Parliament.

In response to their protest the Speaker of the House of Commons ruled that Plimsoll had committed a breach of Parliamentary privilege in contempt of the House – a very serious offence indeed.

In an apologetic speech Plimsoll replied that he had committed the offence unintentionally and that he deeply regretted it; nothing, he explained, had ever been further from his mind than to fail in the respect due to the House, of which he felt it a privilege to be a Member. His apology was accepted, but it did not satisfy everyone, for it was addressed to Mr Speaker and the House, and not to the ship-owning

M.P.s whom he had allegedly attacked, but, as the Prime Minister pointed out, that question could be settled 'elsewhere'.

So indeed it was, for two of the M.P.s brought an action against him on the very grave charge of criminal libel. As his accusations had been unfounded and the M.P.s were known to be men of integrity, their actions seemed likely to succeed.

Plimsoll was seriously alarmed; he now realised, a little late in the day, that before being so free with his accusations he should have made certain of his facts. If he were found guilty he might have to pay heavy damages as well as the costs of the trial and, worse still, other ship-owners might be encouraged to bring actions against him, so that the damages and costs would mount up until he was ruined. He knew from experience what poverty meant, and now both he and his wife might be forced to face this.

Fortunately he had many sympathisers who felt that though he had acted unwisely he had had good intentions and a splendid cause. When some unknown friend opened a Plimsoll Defence Fund to help meet the costs of his trial, many people subscribed to it. Some of Lloyd's under-writers opened a separate fund, not to help meet his costs but to assist his work for the seamen; this showed that although they disapproved of wild accusations against honest shipowners they sympathised with his aims.

After a long and complicated trial the judges decided that although one of the aggrieved owner's vessels had happened to sink through being overloaded, he had not been guilty of habitually overloading them. While not convicting Plimsoll of criminal libel or awarding damages against him, they ordered him to pay his own costs. This cleared the shipowner's name without causing Plimsoll any serious harm, and the other firms who might have brought an action against him realised that it would be hardly worth while to do so.

The result, and indeed the trial itself, brought useful publicity to his book. In spite of its faults, it included many truthful accounts of disasters caused by unseaworthy vessels or by overloading, and thus many of its readers understood how unsatisfactory the laws regulating such matters were. When news came of further disasters they were regarded much more seriously, and aroused more indignation than they would have done but for Plimsoll and his book.

One crew, for example, had been sentenced to twelve weeks' imprisonment, for refusing to sail in an unseaworthy ship. Manned by another crew she left harbour – and within two days she had sunk with all hands. The imprisoned seamen had thereupon been released, for it was clear that if that vessel had been properly inspected they would never have gone to prison, nor would the second crew have met their deaths.

In 1874 another election was held and Plimsoll addressed his constituents in fiery speeches denouncing unseaworthy and overloaded ships and describing his plans: he meant to go to Parliament, he declared, to represent not only Derby but also Britain's seamen. Again he was elected, and though his party, the Liberals, were now in opposition, this did not prevent him putting forward his Shipping Survey Bill. This aimed at stopping cargoes from being carried on deck during the winter, at having all ships surveyed and passed as fit to sail before being allowed to leave harbour, and at insisting on their hulls being plainly marked with load-lines.

His Bill was criticised, even by Members who were as anxious for the welfare of Britain's seamen as he was himself. Some thought that it had been taken too far and might drive much of Britain's trade abroad; some thought that it did not go far enough; and others considered that it was good but that it had been introduced at an inappropriate time. Plimsoll realised that the general feeling of the House was against him, and his Bill was in fact defeated, but only by three votes.

That disappointment was soon succeeded by another, for the Royal Commission on Unseaworthy Ships decided that very little needed to be altered. It pointed out that the Board of Trade already had power to deal with such ships, and expressed the hope that their owners would soon break them up. Moreover, it declared that a load-line would be likely to do more harm than good, for no such line could suit every type of ship. It also decided that there was no point in trying to control overloading; it was for the shipowner or his manager to decide how much cargo his vessels could safely carry.

Plimsoll was furious, especially as he continued to find fresh evidence that 'rotten ships' were still going to sea, that some ships, though apparently quite sound, were built of iron plates so brittle that they would shatter at a blow, and that others were adorned with 'devils' – sham rivets that seemed to hold the plates together without actually doing so. When he found that the Government intended to postpone discussion of the Shipping Bill which he had introduced he lost all self-control.

Beginning quietly, but gradually giving vent to his anger, he told Parliament that some shipowners were little better than 'ship knackers', meaning that they deliberately bought useless vessels because they were cheap. By this time he was not satisfied merely to imply which M.P.s he meant, he actually denounced one of them by name as an example of 'these villains who send sailors to death'.

This unparliamentary language naturally evoked a roar of protest, and the Speaker asked him to withdraw it. When Plimsoll refused he was ordered to leave the House, but it was clear that he was on the verge of a nervous breakdown and hardly responsible for his words; later, his friends said, he might regret them.

When re-admitted a week later, Plimsoll, who was now quite calm, apologised 'frankly and sincerely' for using such language. Again it was obvious that his apology was addressed only to Mr. Speaker and the House, and not to the Member whom he had denounced, but nevertheless it was accepted. Everybody realised that he was still over-wrought and that his outburst was solely due to his concern for the seamen so they were glad to settle the distressing matter.

Unpleasant as it was, however, this scene in the House resulted in much helpful publicity and increased the public demand for protection of seamen. The Government accordingly rushed through the Unseaworthy Ships Bill of 1875.

Although this made the load-line compulsory, it did not impose any penalty if a vessel were loaded so heavily that the line was submerged, nor even state where it was to be marked – indeed, one Welsh skipper showed his contempt for the whole thing by painting his ship's load-line on the funnel! To discover what effect it had had, Plimsoll, who was thoroughly dissatisfied with the Act, visited a number of European ports where British ships were moored and, as he had expected, he found that it had made very little difference.

His wife hoped that the travelling would do him good, for he was obviously ill owing to overwork, but during the journey his health broke down completely and he was forced to return home. As soon as he was well enough he was again in Parliament, pleading for the seamen and improving the Amending Act (to the Unseaworthy Ships Act) before it was passed in 1876.

Plimsoll was not yet satisfied, but his health was so poor that he had to become less active, and in 1879 he somehow injured his right eye so badly that it had to be removed. A year later he gave up his seat in the House of Commons, but not his efforts for the seamen; other Members, he explained, would work for them in Parliament, while he continued to work for them outside.

In 1880 he and his wife hoped to improve their health by a voyage to Australia. There, however, she died, so he returned sadly to Britain with their adopted daughter – they had no children of their own. Five years later he married again. Although his second wife, Harriet Wade, was nearly thirty years younger than himself, they and their six children were quite happy.

Though he could no longer do much for the seamen, they had not forgotten his previous efforts to help them. When Havelock Wilson founded the National Amalgamated Sailors' and Firemen's Union in 1887, it was appropriate that the 'Sailor's Friend', Samuel Plimsoll, should become its first President. He took no part in its business affairs, however, nor in its disputes with the shipowners; apart from presiding at its annual meeting, his chief duty was to advise the Union in its dealings with Parliament.

Wilson was imprisoned for organising a seamen's strike and later he became M.P. for Middlesbrough. He found Plimsoll's experience and advice very useful, and working together, they helped to persuade Parliament to pass the Seaman's Inspection of Provisions Bill, regulating the type of food issued to the crews on board ship.

In 1890 Plimsoll denounced the cruelties practised on the live cargo of the cattle-ships, and as before he made his words more forceful by illustrating them with horrifying photographs. When one of these cattle-ships sank with all hands through being overloaded, he tried to induce her owners to compensate the bereaved relatives of her crew. This was almost his last effort on behalf of the seamen and their dependants, for now he was too old and weak to do more.

On learning that the history books used in the American schools were so unfairly written that they prejudiced the children against Britain, he made one final effort. Hoping to achieve better understanding between the peoples of both countries, he made a special journey to the United States.

Towards the end of his life, wishing to spend his last days near the sea, he moved to Folkestone. It was there that he died on 3rd June 1898 and there that he is buried, the headstone of his grave having an unusual shape, a circle crossed by a horizontal line.

In 1929 as a result of the efforts of his friend Havelock Wilson, a monument was erected to Plimsoll in the Embankment Gardens by the side of the Thames and another stands on the Avon in his birthplace, Bristol. Above all, his achievement is commemorated by the sign borne by the world's shipping – the same sign as marks his grave in Folkestone cemetery: the circle crossed by the horizontal line – the load-line which indicates the depth to which a vessel may be safely immersed. Because he did so much towards its introduction it is almost always known as the Plimsoll Line.

Homes for Children

DR BARNARDO
(1845–1905)

MUCH action had been taken to improve conditions for the children in the mines and factories, but little for the children in the city streets. In the late nineteenth century there was no National Society for the Prevention of Cruelty to Children to protect them, and many suffered not only from cruelty but also from neglect. Even kind-hearted parents were often too poor or ignorant or feckless to look after them, and some children did not even know who their parents were. There were of course orphan asylums, but they were most unpleasant places; so were the prisons, to which a child might be sent for 'vagrancy', the crime of sleeping out in the open.

Even more frail than Louis Braille or Rowland Hill, Thomas John Barnardo, who was born in Dublin on 4th July 1845, was so puny that the doctor doubted whether he would live. When he was about two the poor child was nearly buried alive; his breathing and heart-beats seemed to have stopped, and he had been certified as dead. Fortunately, just as he was being lifted into the coffin, his heart began to beat very feebly, and so his life was saved.

Despite his bad health he was an unruly and careless schoolboy. The only sport he enjoyed was swimming, and the only subject he cared for was reading. He could study when he wished, but he very seldom wished. This infuriated his schoolmaster, whom Barnardo later described as 'one of the biggest and most brutal of bullies . . . He seemed to have a savage delight in beating his boys'. But beatings and bullyings did not cow Thomas Barnardo; instead they instilled into him a life-long hatred of cruelty.

When he entered his father's fur-trading business, after a few terms at College, he turned over a new leaf and became thorough and efficient. His one weakness was that he was rather particular about his clothing; because of some eye-trouble he had to wear unsightly blue spectacles and this made him self-conscious. He might have had a successful career in commerce had not something happened which changed his whole outlook.

He had for some time been opposed to religion, but in 1862 he attended a revival meeting, and was converted to a deep and lasting faith in Christianity. He burned the irreligious books that had formerly delighted him and read the Bible in real earnest; he joined the Open Plymouth Brethren, of which his brothers were members, and began to devote all his spare time to religious work.

When he led a Bible Class at one of Dublin's Ragged Schools he found the children so difficult to control that for a time he was tempted to hit them with his walking-stick. The next time he avoided this temptation by leaving his stick at home and he was surprised to find that he could keep order simply by kindness. His work with the children led him to visit their homes and he was horrified by the dreadful conditions in the Dublin slums.

He was successful not only with children but with adults. He held Bible classes for the local police and troops, hired a room in which he could hold his own revival meetings, and went from house to house through the slums, inviting the people to join him in prayer. He gave them tracts (religious booklets) and, if they were old and poverty-stricken, packets of tea.

This work alone did not satisfy Barnardo: he wanted to devote not merely his spare time but his whole life to spreading Christianity. When at a religious meeting he heard about the need for mission workers in China, he decided that here lay the task for him. Next day he left his father's business and within two months he went to London to train himself for the mission field.

He had hoped to set out for China almost at once, but medical missionaries were so badly needed that he agreed, very reluctantly, to spend three years studying to qualify as a doctor. While in training at the London Hospital in Whitechapel, he was appalled to find that the slums nearby were even worse than those of Dublin. To add to his distress he was so serious-minded that he did not get on well with the other students, who, though good-hearted, were sportive and rowdy.

London was then so unhealthy a place that diseases spread rapidly and an epidemic of cholera, which occurred soon after his arrival, swept through the overcrowded slums like wild-fire. He and the other students had to visit the houses to tend the sick, finding only too often that there was nothing they could do. Barnardo, however, realised that there was always something he could do: if he could not save a dying man he could at least pray by his bedside, and he could also understand the dreadful conditions in which so many people lived and died. 'But for that epidemic I should never have known Stepney and all its horrors,' he declared afterwards.

Being a member of the Plymouth Brethren, he spent all his spare time holding prayer-meetings in the streets or going into the public houses to sell copies of the Bible. Neither ridicule nor violence dismayed him, nor would he ever retaliate. When he was so fiercely attacked that two of his ribs were broken he refused to prosecute the louts who had assaulted him, and when the children in his Ragged School dropped him out of the window, he calmly walked in through the door and went on teaching them. This gave him great influence over the young people; those responsible for breaking his ribs called every day at his lodgings to inquire after his health, and when one night he found that six of the toughest boys in his class were following him, they explained that it was to protect him from a hooligan who had threatened to attack him.

A few of his fellow medical students were equally impressed by his courage and devotion, and two of them helped him to run his combined Sunday and evening school. They had to begin by cleaning and white-washing the rough shed in which it was held, and then deal with a crowd of ragged and dirty street-urchins.

One evening, after the school had closed, Barnardo noticed a small

boy crouching by the fire. 'Please, sir, let me stop!' the child pleaded earnestly. He explained that he had no home and no parents. He had escaped from the workhouse and been sent to prison for vagrancy, and he had no wish to return to either. But he knew how to find shelter in the London streets, in a barrel, under a tarpaulin, or in a gutter of a roof, anywhere out of sight of the police. On his lucky nights he might find a bed in a hay-cart. In spite of his experience of the London slums, Barnardo had not realised that there were any homeless children, and the idea disturbed him. After giving the boy a much-needed meal he asked to be taken to find other orphans.

A walk through some very unpleasant slums brought them to the foot of a wall in Petticoat Lane.

'But where are the boys?' Barnardo asked a little impatiently.

'Up there, sir – up that wall,' the boy told him.

They climbed the wall, and on the roof above it they saw in the moonlight eleven boys huddled together for warmth, barefooted, wretchedly clad and looking half-starved, yet asleep in spite of their hunger and the cold. 'And there's lots more lays like this,' the boy assured him.

Barnardo at once decided that something must be done to improve conditions for such children. But what could he, a poor medical student, due to sail for China in a year or so, do? There was only one answer: he must find a home for the boy who had guided him and later arrange for him to emigrate to Canada to become a farmer.

When he described this experience at a Missionary Conference it was widely reported in the press and many people were equally horrified. One of them was Lord Shaftesbury; he too felt it hard to believe that there were homeless children in London and asked Barnardo to show him some.

Together they went to a corner where some large tarpaulins covered a number of barrels and crates. There were no signs of any children, but Barnardo noticed a gap between two of the tarpaulins. Thrusting in his hand, he hauled out a very scared, small boy.

There were plenty of other boys beneath the tarpaulins, but they were so frightened that they refused to come out until they had been promised a meal and a penny each. When they heard some coins jingle on the pavement they swarmed out, seventy-three ragged and barefoot 'street arabs', as Lord Shaftesbury called them. As he watched them wolfing their meal he decided that 'all London must know about this', and he urged Barnardo to push on with his work.

An appeal for help which Barnardo published in a religious paper brought little response, but in spite of this he was able in 1867 to open a Sunday-school in an East End public house. Within a few months, however, a new landlord, who did not sympathise with his work, took over, and the school had to close – a disappointment which caused Barnardo to suffer a nervous breakdown.

The next year, as soon as he had recovered, he started the East End Juvenile Mission in two small cottages joined to make one. He provided books for children who could read and had them read to those who could not; he organised sewing classes for the girls from a match-factory and he found jobs for the more reliable teenagers and encouraged them to save. He still felt religious teaching to be the most important part of his work but, as before, that only occupied his spare time; he continued to train to become a doctor.

Now he had to make a difficult decision: whether he should go to China as he had planned, or, as Lord Shaftesbury suggested, stay in Britain and work among London's street arabs. He could remember how at one public meeting a poor servant girl had given him a package containing twenty-seven farthings, all she had been able to save out of her scanty wages: she had meant it, she explained, for foreign missions, but now she thought it ought to go to the 'poor heathen at home'.

A surprise gift of a thousand pounds from a total stranger for his work in the slums made him decide that when he had passed his medical exams he would devote all his time to the children. He acquired two more cottages, and by constructing a roof over their backyards he built a hall large enough to hold three hundred people. This enabled him to hold classes every day, some of the teachers being qualified school-masters and schoolmistresses, and he provided cheap, or free, dinners for the poorest pupils. His kindness, combined with the religious teaching he gave them, converted many a loutish boy and sluttish girl into a decent self-respecting young person.

Yet he was not satisfied, for what would happen to them when school was over, when some had to return to squalid homes and live with brutal or drunken adults? What they really needed was a *home*, and he determined to provide one, for the boys at any rate.

In 1870 he was able to rent a large house in Stepney Causeway; toiling to make it habitable, he invited his wealthy friends to visit it, hoping that they would subscribe to its cost. Many, among whom was Lord Shaftesbury, did so, enabling him to provide accommodation large enough for about sixty boys, with bathrooms and toilets, a kitchen and wash-house, and quarters for the 'father and mother' who were to run the Home.

Generous though his friends had been, Barnardo could at first take only twenty-five boys, whom he chose from among the poorest and most wretched of the street arabs. On admission they had to be bathed and de-loused, but the clothes of some were so grimed to their bodies that they had first to be soaked, boy as well, in warm water and the rags peeled off. Then the boys were given new clothes and were ready to be brought up decently.

When he had found work for five boys outside the Home, to avoid getting into debt Barnardo would admit only five others to take their place. Even when a small boy followed him, pleading earnestly to be allowed in, he felt that he could not afford to accept him at once; instead he promised to do so as soon as he had a vacancy and gave him a few pence. A few days later he heard that this very boy had died of exhaustion, caused by exposure and lack of food.

Barnardo was appalled. He resolved that, debt or no debt, such a thing must never happen again. Over the entrance to his home he placed a notice which read:

NO DESTITUTE CHILD IS EVER REFUSED ADMISSION

Thanks to the help the public gave him he did not have to wait for boys to come along: he went out to look for them. Night after night he visited the slums seeking for them. Some were ready to enter the Home at once but others refused; an Education Act was now in force and the children were as scared of school as they were of prison. When Barnardo found a boy who boasted that he preferred freedom, he gave him the Home's address and told him to think it over, hoping that when he had thought it over, the boy might be quite ready to come in.

Barnardo sought for boys in markets, fairs and factories, and on Epsom Racecourse on Derby Day. He even slept in one of the worst of the common lodging-houses – or he tried to do so, but the vermin drove him away. One dark night he was waylaid and robbed, but before long his money and watch were returned; had the hooligans realised who he was, they explained apologetically, they would never have dreamed of robbing him.

Kind though he was, Barnardo was never deceived by boys who were not as poor as they suggested. He questioned all applicants for admission, but if he had to refuse a boy because he was not really destitute, he tried to help him in other ways, perhaps by finding him a job where he could 'live in'.

Needless to say, he ran his Home on religious lines, with prayers, Bible-reading and hymns, and while he was concerned for the boys' souls he also provided plenty of activities to develop their bodies and minds. Rising early, they helped with the everyday work of the Home; they spent the weekday mornings in school and the afternoons learning a trade. They played games in the yard, where a drill sergeant also gave them physical training; they wore a smart uniform and had their own band. Punishments, when necessary, were not too severe, and Barnardo insisted that the Home was to be run by kindness.

Some of the boys were enrolled in the 'Limehouse Shoeblack Brigade', and others in a 'City Messenger Brigade', running errands, delivering circulars and so forth; others supplied householders with firewood; others, the 'Busy Bees', made boots and shoes and brushes. The money these boys earned helped to run the Home.

In 1873 Barnardo had to enlarge his Home, for his 'family' had grown to 130; and now he added another sign, so that no destitute boy need fear being turned away at any time:

OPEN ALL NIGHT

He had also set up another Ragged School; he was finding work for boys as apprentices and for girls in domestic service, and was arranging for some of the older boys to emigrate to Canada.

This work was very expensive, and the amount that the boys earned did not by any means meet it. Barnardo relied chiefly on what he called 'prayer and appeal', and many of his prayers were answered. He lectured and wrote in religious and other papers about conditions in the slums, interesting and touching the hearts of his readers and thus making them anxious to help.

Realising, as had Shaftesbury, how much evil was caused by drunkenness, he signed the pledge himself and invited others to do so by erecting a 'temperance tent' outside one of the roughest of London's public houses. As before, he and his followers were jeered at and attacked, but again his steadfastness impressed even his enemies, and some time later he was able to buy the tavern itself. Then he re-opened the *Edinburgh Castle* as a combined 'People's Church' and 'Coffee Palace', where callers could purchase a hot non-alcoholic drink, cheap wholesome meals, and receive a warm welcome. Though he personally disapproved of tobacco and did not like games, he provided a smoking-room for the men (women did not smoke in those days) and a games-room. He held regular Services, attendance at which was voluntary, and tried to visit all the members of his 'congregation', which numbered about two thousand.

In 1873 he married Syrie Louise Elmslie. He had first met her two years before at a tea-party she was giving for her own Ragged School, so she sympathised greatly with his work. Her well-to-do parents naturally wished the wedding to take place in a fashionable church near their home; but they gave way to Barnardo, who was anxious to have it held in a famous London nonconformist church, the Metropolitan Tabernacle. This was large enough to hold not only the bride's family and friends but the crowds of his many poor friends from East London.

As a married man with a growing family, he had to give more thought to earning a living than he had hitherto done; he did so by writing articles for the newspapers, collecting material full of human interest from his own experiences. While it raised this problem, his marriage solved another; he and his wife could now open a Home for girls.

Their first venture was not a success; they tried to run it too much on the lines of the other Homes, but they found that methods that worked well for boys were not suitable for girls. After much anxious thought, Barnardo realised that what they needed was not one large Home but a small village of cottage homes, each holding about twenty girls, with a 'mother' who could give them some idea of family life. This would, of course, be expensive – and he wondered how the money could be raised.

As usual, he tried prayer and appeal; and again his prayers were answered. One morning a complete stranger knocked on the door of his room in a hotel.

'Is your name Barnardo?' he asked. 'You are thinking of building a village for little girls? Then you will want some cottages – have you got any? Not yet? Well, put me down for the first cottage. Good morning.' And then the stranger walked away.

Hurrying after him, Barnardo learned that the man's only daughter had recently died, and that he and his wife were anxious to erect a memorial to her, but had been uncertain what form it should take. They had heard of the scheme for a Village Home and when the stranger found that he and Barnardo were actually staying in the same hotel, he regarded this as a sign from Providence.

Reading about this donation in a religious paper, several other people also offered cottages, often as a memorial to dead relatives or friends. In 1875 the Village was opened near Ilford, in Essex: it consisted of twenty-five cottages, each with four large bedrooms for the girls, a

playroom, kitchen and scullery and so forth, and quarters for the 'mother'. Her work was to make the girls under her charge feel like one large family, to watch over their health, to give them religious ideals, to teach them ordinary household duties, and to train them as domestic servants – there was then hardly any other suitable work which the Barnardo's would have cared for them to undertake. These homes were as much a success as the rest of Dr Barnardo's work.

He had now opened yet another Ragged School, a second Coffee Palace, an evening club and the first of London's cabmen's shelters. His work was widely renowned, and he had made many friends in all walks of life – policemen, public-house keepers, and peers.

Unfortunately he had also made a few enemies, and among those was another society which was striving, though not so effectively, to help the poor, and which was jealous of his success. Barnardo found himself accused in the press of half-starving and ill-treating the children under his care, of punishing them harshly, of neglecting their health and their religious welfare, and of using money given to the Homes for his own benefit.

He replied to these accusations by writing calm reasonable letters to the press. This did not satisfy his attackers, and the jealous society put his Homes on their 'Cautionary List', denouncing them as being unworthy of public support.

If he had brought a libel action against his accusers they would have had to pay heavy damages, but his faith as a Plymouth Brother forbade him to take legal action, and he would have scorned making money in such an unpleasant way. Instead he referred the matter to arbitration, an official investigation held by responsible people. After examining a number of witnesses, making full inquiries, and inspecting the Homes, the arbitrators decided that, apart from one minor detail in which he had acted unwisely, there was no truth in the charges brought against him, and their report completely cleared his name:

> We are of opinion that these Homes for Destitute Boys and Girls, called the 'Barnardo Institutions', are real and valuable charities, and worthy of public support and confidence.

The Homes were speedily removed from that 'Cautionary List', and their work was much helped by the publicity resulting from this decision. Barnardo welcomed it, but the whole unhappy affair had told badly on his health, and he was in grave danger of another, and more serious nervous breakdown.

The arbitrators had recommended that the Homes should be supervised by a committee of influential people who would not only command public respect but take a helpful interest in the work. Barnardo gladly agreed, and he was delighted when one of Britain's most influential people volunteered to become its Chairman: the Lord Chancellor of England.

For some time Dr Barnardo had been editing two magazines. One, meant for young readers, aimed at giving religious ideals while at the same time being full of interest and excitement. It contained a serial and articles on hobbies and natural history, and held competitions, mostly on Biblical subjects.

The other, written for adults, described the work of the Homes and explained the need for it, giving well-illustrated details of the terrible suffering which so many of the slum children had to endure. It also enabled Barnardo to appeal to his readers for gifts not only of money but of toys, bedding, material for making clothes for the girls, Christmas presents, and so forth.

The magazines were so successful that he opened his own publishing house in the Strand, with a reading-room and a young people's library, containing not only books specially written for children but adult books which boys and girls could enjoy. He travelled round the country giving public lectures, and appealed through the papers for help with the further projects he was planning.

The help arrived, enabling Barnardo to rebuild and enlarge the first Boys' Home he had opened, and to provide an infirmary, also in Stepney, for sick children, a convalescent home in Sussex, a home in Jersey for boys under ten, and a clinic for free medical service in the East End. He arranged for his Ragged Schools to give a free breakfast and a cheap but nourishing dinner to any poor child who seemed in need of a good meal; and where poor parents were unable to send their children to school because they had no boots for them to wear, he would supply these. His wife helped him by addressing public meetings herself and writing to the press; she organised a Deaconess service, with a centre at Bow where ladies could be trained to visit the poor and to find out how they most needed help.

Now he had personal troubles to face; leaving the Plymouth Brethren, he joined the Church of England, and this estranged him from two of his brothers, who felt that they could no longer welcome him into their homes. He also had so many expenses to meet that, in 1883, he very reluctantly had to appeal to the Trustees of his Homes for a salary, which they gave gladly.

He had also to face another difficulty, that of finding work for the young people when they became too old to stay in the Homes. Already Barnardo had sent hundreds of them to what were then called the Colonies, but only singly or in pairs. In 1882 he began organising systematic emigration, the first batch of fifty-one boys going to Quebec. They were welcomed so warmly and got on so well that he was able to send boys and girls over by hundreds, and he went over himself to see how they were progressing – very nicely, he found; though the Canadian authorities had become wary of British emigrants, some of whom were young criminals, they seldom had any fault to find with any of those whom he sent out.

Ill due to overwork, in 1885 he had to take a holiday on the Riviera, but he was soon pining to return from the warm sunshine to the gloom and damp of the London streets; neither ill-health nor his distress when two of his children died could keep him long from his work. Shortly after his return he opened what he called a 'Babies' Castle', and a special home for girls suffering so badly from nerve trouble that they could not mix with other children, and he arranged for some of the children to be boarded out with suitable families.

In 1887 Barnardo celebrated Queen Victoria's Golden Jubilee by again enlarging the Stepney Home for Boys and his Children's Infirmary, and by adding more cottages to the Girls' Village Home. During the following year he opened two lodging houses for children at a charge of a penny a night – or free if the child could not afford even that.

Overworked, ill, and harassed by arguments with well-meaning people who misunderstood his ideals, he supervised the running of all his Homes; he again visited Canada to see how his young emigrants were faring and he started new schemes and raised funds to pay for them. Yet, however busy he was with office work and public appeals, he always retained a personal interest in the boys and girls in the Homes, and was very distressed when ill-health prevented him from visiting the docks as was his custom, to see a group of his young emigrants when they set off for Canada.

His health was failing: he was suffering from a fatal heart-disease, but the knowledge that the end might come at any time only spurred him on to work harder. At last came the final heart-attack, and 'the father of nobody's children' died on 19th September 1905.

For three days he 'lay in state' at the Edinburgh Castle, the inn which he had converted into a coffee-house and a People's Church; tens of thousands of mourners filed by, and in the East End many a flag flew at half-mast. Then, as he had wished, his body was cremated and the ashes were buried in the grounds of the Girls' Village Homes.

Today his work is still going on, not only in the famous Barnardo Homes – there are over a hundred in the British Isles, ten in Australia and one in Kenya – but in the lives of the thousands whom he had rescued from the slums, brought up in decent surroundings and given a new start in life. The first of his Boys' Homes in Stepney Causeway is now the headquarters from which the work is carried out, and here the notice is still displayed:

NO DESTITUTE CHILD IS EVER REFUSED ADMISSION.

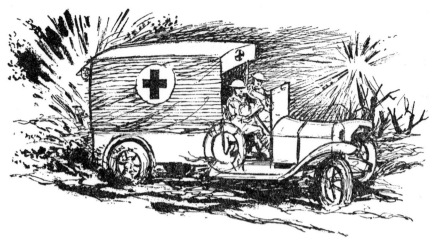

The Red Cross

JEAN HENRI DUNANT
(1828–1910)

WHETHER fought with bows and arrows or with hydrogen bombs, wars are bound to inflict terrible injuries. This has always aroused the sympathy of good-hearted people, some of whom have willingly incurred great risks to tend the wounded. Until recent years, however, the first aid and hospital services were not very efficient, and often dealt only with their own army's casualties, leaving the enemy's wounded to suffer.

Geneva, the capital of Switzerland, has long had a fine reputation for its ideals of freedom and honesty in business. It was there that Jean Henri Dunant was born on 8th May 1828.

His parents taught him their religious faith and made him value strict honesty. While he was quite young he showed that he had a sympathetic nature, and the fable about the wolf and the lamb distressed him greatly. 'No, he mustn't eat the lamb!' he wailed. 'I won't have him eat the lamb!' He was comforted when his mother assured him that it was only a story and that it had happened long ago, but as he grew older he realised that there are human wolves and lambs in real life, and in modern times.

When he was six, his family visited a relative in the South of France, and Jean Henri's father, whose work included prison welfare, took him to see the convict station at Toulon. As he watched the men aimlessly shuffling about the prison yard, and working in their chains at road-making, the poor child was horrified. 'When I'm big I'll write a book to save them!' he vowed, and the memory of their suffering long haunted his dreams.

After leaving school to work in a bank, he remembered his vow and tried to bring a little hope and happiness into the town prison by visiting the convicts every Sunday to talk to them and read from the Bible and from interesting travel books. As an earnest member of a Protestant revivalist mission, he diligently studied the Bible; believing that the strange dreams and visions in the Book of Daniel were prophecies, he tried to read them as forecasts of events in his own time.

When he was about nineteen a civil war broke out in Switzerland between Catholics and Protestants. Fortunately the government troops had a humane commander, who ordered his men not to injure the civilians or destroy any places of worship, but to treat their prisoners considerately, to tend the enemy wounded as well as their own, and to avoid reprisals of any kind. This impressed Dunant, making him realise that even wars might avoid unnecessary suffering, and that they could be settled reasonably, allowing people of widely different outlook to live together in peace.

Some years later he was delighted when Mrs Harriet Beecher Stowe, author of *Uncle Tom's Cabin*, visited Geneva and he was permitted to meet her. At first he felt rather disappointed – she seemed so very ordinary – but when she began to describe how the slaves suffered and to explain the need for setting them free, he was filled with enthusiasm. He spoke of her as a 'saint', and resolved that he too would do all he could to help free them.

Some of the Protestant organisations in France, Belgium, and Switzerland were then trying to form a French-speaking union. This did not satisfy Dunant, who proposed instead that the Young Men's Christian Associations of all lands should unite in a great, world-wide brotherhood. His suggestion led, in 1855, to the formation of the World's Alliance of Y.M.C.A.s.

In 1853, the bank for which he worked had sent him to one of its subsidiary companies in Algeria. Dunant, who was impressed with the country's possibilities, formed his own company for developing it. Meanwhile he wrote a book contrasting the slavery he saw around him with slavery in the United States and decided that, on the whole, the former was the more tolerable.

His scheme for developing Algeria did not prosper, and after many unavailing efforts to save those who had invested in his company from being ruined, he realised that he must appeal personally to the Emperor of France, Napoleon III, for Algeria then belonged to France.

He had chosen an unfortunate time, for in that year, 1859, Napoleon, anxious to free Italy from Austrian rule, had declared war on Austria, and had himself gone to the front in Northern Italy. Dunant decided to follow him, and after some difficulty in crossing the Apennine Mountains he succeeded in reaching the French headquarters. The high-ranking officers were greatly surprised by the sudden arrival of a civilian in white tropical kit; this, Dunant thought, would make an effective contrast to their uniforms.

The officers were still more amazed when he tried to arouse their sympathy for the casualties in the previous victories. 'What do you expect?' one of the generals asked him. 'After all, you can't make an omelette without breaking eggs!' But if the visitor really wanted to see a first-class battle, he added, he should go back across the Apennines.

This was more difficult than before, because the route was through regions devastated by the fighting. As, however, the driver of Dunant's carriage was a deserter, he knew the way to the battlefield which was to the south of Lake Garda. It included a number of villages and farms around a town and a tower-crowned hill, both called Solferino.

Although the French commander was using Montgolfier (hot air) balloons* to observe the enemy, the outbreak of the battle on 24th June 1859 took both armies by surprise. About 3 a.m. the French advanced, but it was not until they reached the Austrian outposts that the fighting began in real earnest. They progressed across very difficult country, through a barrage of shells and war-rockets, and both armies met in a headlong charge. Soon they were engaged in hand-to-hand conflict, fighting not only with bayonets and rifle-butts but with stones and bare fists and even with their teeth. The very horses, maddened by the tumult, attacked and bit one another, while their riders slashed and

* See *Inventors of the World* pp. 51–62.

95

stabbed with their sabres. The cavalry charged, and the artillery rattled across the battlefield, crushing wounded and dying beneath their hooves and wheels. Round every strong-point, every mound and ridge, farm and village, the fighting was especially fierce.

The Austrian army was already beginning to retreat when, at about five in the afternoon, the weather put an end to the battle. An extremely hot day was followed by a terrific gale, accompanied by a cloud-burst of rain and hail which swept along a cloud of blinding dust, and the darkness was broken only by the flashes of lightning.

At first intermittently, and then all along the line, the fighting ceased. The Austrian retreat became a rout: the French had triumphed and Italy was free – or at least part of it was. Shocked at the casualties, Napoleon and the Austrian Emperor had agreed to a compromise peace.

There had been many acts of extraordinary heroism, when the troops fought to save or recapture their tattered bloodstained colours, and when dying officers asked to be held on their feet to give their last orders. There had been acts of needless cruelty, when no quarter was given and some of the wounded had been mercilessly slain. But there had also been acts of mercy, when officers forbade their men to fire on their wounded enemies and when the canteen women, under heavy fire, took drinking-water to the suffering men.

After a night of horror, during which the wearied troops tried to give their injured comrades what little help they could, next morning the battlefield was strewn for miles with dead bodies and with wounded and dying men. To add to the horror, looters were robbing the dead and wounded, and a few of the peasants hired to bury the dead bodies were so callous or hasty that some of the wounded were flung into their graves while still alive.

Though unable to cope with the heavy casualties, the overworked members of the French medical services did their utmost to tend them and take them to safety. Neither did they forget the splendid tradition of their country, for they cared for the enemy wounded as well as their own. 'What a nation you French are!' a general captured in another battle had said. 'You fight like lions, and once you have beaten your enemies you treat them as though they were your best friends!'

The small town of Castiglione, not far from the battlefield, became

the chief collecting-centre for the wounded. For three days they were
brought in, in such numbers that they had to be crowded together in
the churches and other buildings, in rough shelters hurriedly built in
the streets, and in the homes of the townspeople, who willingly gave
them all the bedding and linen for bandages that they could spare. The
people did all they could for them, but they were overwhelmed by the
numbers and unnerved by the sight of so much suffering. When a false
alarm that the Austrian army was coming back was raised, a panic
arose in which some of the wounded were more severely injured.

Then the townsfolk and the doctors and patients were amazed to
see a total stranger busily organising a first-aid service. Though
nobody knew who he was, this was no time to ask questions, and he was
so competent that his instructions were obeyed. The wounded soldiers
simply called him 'the man in white'.

It was Dunant, still wearing his tropical kit, going into the churches
where the sufferers lay, tending their injuries, giving them food and

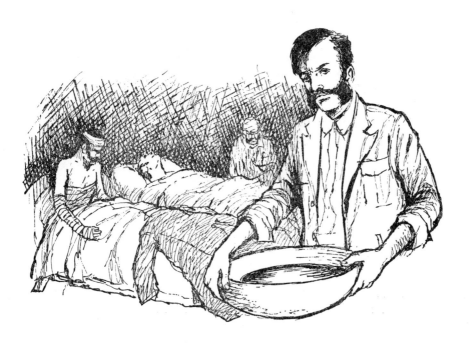

drink and tobacco – the smoke was thought to be a disinfectant – acting as interpreter, trying to comfort the dying, and writing down their messages for home. He heartened the women and girls of Castiglione to renewed efforts, organised them into a volunteer nursing service, and sent them to wash the sufferers' wounds and to supply them with drinking-water which the boys and younger children brought from the well. He told them to make no distinction between enemy and friend: '*Tutti fratelli*,' he reminded them. 'All men are brothers.' He obtained food and herbal remedies from a neighbouring town, and induced casual visitors and tourists to help with the work.

Some of these amateur nurses were so sickened by the great suffering which they could do so little to relieve that before long they had to give up. Needless to say, Dunant was not one of them! He toiled on unflaggingly until order was achieved from chaos and until arrangements could be made to transport some of the wounded to the neighbouring villages and towns. Their places were soon taken by others.

When he did leave Castiglione for a few days, it was simply to travel, again at the risk of his life, to the French headquarters. Unable to speak with Napoleon, he sent him a message, urging him to release the captured Austrian doctors so that they could help tend the wounded. Napoleon needed little urging; he was still horrified at the suffering his victory had caused.

Dunant then returned to his work in the hospitals, again acting as interpreter and again reminding the helpers, '*Tutti fratelli* – all men are brothers.' At last, having done all that he could in Italy and having worn himself out, he returned to Switzerland to rest.

He found himself quite unable to rest; and though he had failed to interest Napoleon in his Algerian project he now had little heart to work on this for he could think of nothing but the sufferings he had witnessed in Italy. He wrote to influential people, and when he visited Paris he pleaded with them, striving to awaken their sympathy for the war-wounded. They paid little attention to his pleas, however, and soon he felt that they were beginning to get bored with him.

Still, he did have two minor successes. That general who had been so cynical about war casualties now admitted that he was taking them much more seriously, and the scientists of Paris were really interested when Dunant told them the seeming impossibility that the hair of one

Austrian soldier had turned white overnight at Solferino.

At last Dunant could bear it no longer. Returning to Geneva, he isolated himself in a flat near the Cathedral and began to write. He read all the official accounts of the Battle of Solferino, studied the maps, and had experts to check the details. At last his book was finished: not a large one, but it has thrown a new light on history.

A Memory of Solferino is its title. Not 'memories', Dunant was careful to explain, but simply the one memory that dominated his mind, the memory of the wounded brought into the town. After briefly describing the battle, he dwelt in more detail on the suffering it caused, not piling on the horrors but simply relating the facts and allowing them to speak for themselves. He paid tribute to the work of the townsfolk and other amateur nurses who had served so tirelessly in the hospitals, but he pointed out that it was useless to leave such tasks to good-hearted but untrained people who volunteered after the battle was over. Workers were needed who would take the trouble to train themselves before the war broke out. 'Would it not be possible, in time of peace and quiet,' he asked, 'to form relief societies for the purposes of having care given to the wounded in time of war by zealous, devoted, and thoroughly qualified volunteers?'

Short though his book was, he made it more impressive by having it beautifully produced and printed on good quality paper; this was expensive, but he was in no mood for counting the cost. As he did not intend it to be sold but simply to be given to influential people who might be able to help, only 1600 copies were at first published.

The result surpassed his wildest hopes. His book was read and discussed so widely that he had to have another edition printed, and then another. It was translated into many languages and attracted the attention of influential people in many lands.

Among them was the Swiss lawyer, Dr Gustave Moynier, president of the Geneva Society for Public Welfare. Though less of an enthusiast than Dunant, he was far more practical, and it was as a result of his efforts that the Society appointed them both to a special Committee of Five to study Dunant's proposals – the others were two doctors and that general who had so humanely waged the civil war in Switzerland years before.

After three meetings they decided to become a Permanent International Committee, whose aim was to bind all civilised nations 'by a kind of Covenant' to treat war casualties humanely. Moynier then suggested that they should call an International Conference to meet in Geneva later that year, and invite all civilised nations to send their representatives.

Full of excitement, Dunant travelled round the capitals of Western Europe, again trying to interest influential people in the Conference. Yet its aims, as proposed by Moynier, did not satisfy him: he wanted the wounded, and those who treated them, to be regarded as neutrals; but this annoyed Moynier, who thought that so far-fetched an idea would turn people against the whole scheme.

The Conference, when it met on 26th October 1863, was a complete success. All who attended it realised how important an occasion this was. It was the first time that any sort of international attempt had been made to lessen the horrors of war. Indeed, the very word 'international' was almost new.

Eighteen delegates, from fourteen nations, attended the Conference. Moynier was in the chair, and Dunant was elected Secretary. The Conference decided that each country should form its own society to make arrangements for attending to casualties on the battlefield. There would of course have to be a 'mother committee' to enable them to co-operate, and this work would be carried out in Geneva by the original Committee of Five. The question of treating the wounded and those who tended them as neutral was too important for them to decide; it would have to be settled by the governments themselves in a Diplomatic Conference. The proceedings ended with a vote of thanks to the Geneva Society for the Public Welfare and to Monsieur Dunant, to whose untiring efforts the whole project was due.

The Diplomatic Conference was held on 8th August 1864, and was attended by twenty-six representatives of sixteen countries, including the U.S.A. Moynier was one of its members, but Dunant was not; he was merely allotted the less important task of organising the delegates' entertainments, and he may have felt that he was being frozen out of the great international movement which he had inspired.

He cared little about this, however, and was delighted when the Conference decided that the wounded and the medical services were to be given neutral status. Moreover, as Dunant had suggested earlier, they were to have their own distinctive flag.

As the Conference was held in Switzerland, its members complimented that country by adopting the Swiss Flag, a white cross on a red field, but with its colours reversed. This was the origin of the Red Cross Flag, with its field of white, which is now honoured everywhere as the sign of mercy in war and of help in both war and peace. (Mohammedan countries, however, use the Red Crescent on white, and Persia has its own emblem, the Lion and Sun, also in red on white.)

Dunant had been so busy working for what is now called the Red Cross that he had had little time to spare for his schemes in Africa. These had deteriorated, and nothing he could do would save them. In 1867 they failed completely and he was declared bankrupt. Feeling that this disgraced their town, the people of Geneva deprived him of his citizenship, and he also had to resign his Secretaryship of the International Committee.

Realising that not only was he ruined but that he had done serious harm to those who had invested in his scheme, Dunant felt his position very keenly. He was not comforted when at an Exhibition held in Paris that year, he saw his own bust garlanded with laurel – at a time when he himself was desperately poor and living from hand to mouth! To add to his distress, another International Conference had failed to extend the Geneva Convention to cover naval warfare by using the Red Cross to protect hospital ships.

He was still in Paris when, during the Franco-Prussian War of 1870–1871, the city was besieged and starved into submission by the Germans; the siege was followed by a vicious civil war, resulting in the Paris Commune.

Terrible though these disasters were, they enabled Dunant to continue the work so dear to his heart; he helped manufacture a new form of medicated lint for dressing wounds and sent supplies of this lint and a number of blankets to the troops in the fortifications defending the city. He also arranged lectures and entertainments for them, something on the lines of the modern E.N.S.A.

Later he was able to save a number of Parisians who had offended the authorities and were in danger of imprisonment or death. There was only one railway line by which anyone could leave the city, and for that a passport was essential. Although Geneva had disowned

Dunant, he was still a Swiss citizen, carrying a Swiss passport, so, at grave risks to himself if the trick were discovered, he lent it to these refugees one by one. After they had used it to pass the guards at the fortifications, a friendly railway official would bring it back to him to lend to someone else.

Later he used it himself to get out of the city in an attempt to persuade the Prussians to let the women and children leave Paris. He was unsuccessful, but he tried in other ways to relieve the hardships of the siege; his life was in danger not only from the shelling but from the risk of his being denounced as a spy, for in the fierce fighting which ended the Commune even the Red Cross could give little protection.

Distressed but not discouraged by these experiences, Dunant again strove to obtain more merciful treatment for prisoners of war. He also helped to form the Universal Alliance of Order and Civilisation: its aims were to replace war by a code of international justice and to 'raise the moral and intellectual level of the citizen'.

Such ideas aroused much sympathy in England and Dunant was warmly welcomed when he visited the country in 1872. His hardships in Paris had told upon him so much, however, that his health failed and for a time his right hand was crippled by an attack of eczema. Although he gave a few lectures he was too poor to travel north to lecture, or even to accept an invitation to visit Florence Nightingale, whose work in the Crimean hospitals he had long admired, but he was encouraged by the sympathetic letter which she sent him.

Again living from hand to mouth, but still urging that prisoners of war should be more humanely treated, he attended an international conference in Brussels to discuss this subject, but, as before, it was a failure. He also pleaded for the world-wide abolition of slavery, and worked on another development scheme, this time in the Holy Land, but this again was unsuccessful.

During his visit to London in 1874 he tried to popularise a strange musical instrument which a friend of his had invented, the Pyrophone, in which a number of gas-jets burning in glass tubes produced different musical notes. For a time it seemed likely to become popular, and Jenny Lind, the 'Swedish nightingale', sang to the accompaniment of the 'Singing Flames'. Unfortunately it was not practical, and at last all Dunant could do was to preserve it for posterity by presenting it to the

Science Museum in South Kensington.

With his health failing and his mind still burdened by the knowledge that he was exiled from his own city for bankruptcy, Dunant wandered unhappily through Western Europe, sometimes visiting England and sometimes resting in hospital in Heiden, a small Swiss village. So seldom did he appear in public that most people believed he was dead. His family knew that he was still alive, however, and made him a small allowance in token of the good work which he had done.

*   *   *

Years later, in 1895, a Swiss journalist Georg Baumberger heard that staying in a hospital at Heiden was an old man of whom Switzerland should be proud. Scenting a story, he politely asked for an interview, and to his amazement he found that this old man was the half-forgotten Jean Henri Dunant, the founder of that world-wide organisation, the Red Cross.

In a Swiss paper he told the story of the old man's life and of the hardships he had endured. Soon the story spread far and wide, and the world realised how much it owed to Dunant and how shabbily it had treated him. Fortunately it was not too late to make amends.

Greetings and messages of respect reached Dunant from monarchs, from religious leaders and from the Red Cross Societies of many lands. Generous gifts reached him, too, freeing him from any fear of poverty, and when the Nobel Prizes were first awarded in 1901, half of the Peace Prize was assigned to Dunant, an honour which he valued greatly.

So during his last years he was freed not only from want but from the feeling of disgrace which had so long oppressed him. No longer did Geneva disown him as a bankrupt unworthy of citizenship; its people realised that he had brought not shame but honour upon their town. Most important of all, he rejoiced to learn that in 1899 a Convention at the Hague had achieved something for which he had long worked: it had at last extended to cover the victims of naval warfare, so that the Red Cross could now be displayed at sea.

After his death on 30th October 1910, Dunant was given a very quiet funeral; as one solitary church bell tolled, his body was hauled to the graveyard on a hand-cart by one of his friends, and no other mourners were present. This was not callousness or neglect; he had expressed a wish in his days of lonely bitterness: 'Let me be carried to my grave like a dog.'

Dunant was dead, but all over the world the Red Cross Societies are still continuing his work. As a result of the First World War another of his hopes was fulfilled; rules were laid down for the treatment of prisoners of war, and in 1949 efforts were made to protect civilians in war-time.

The Red Cross, too, functions not only in war but in peace. In local accidents its trained first-aiders are always ready to help, and when there is a great disaster, a famine or a flood, an epidemic of disease or an earthquake, then the International Red Cross, from the Societies of many lands, brings relief to the victims.

Although a representative of Britain had signed the Geneva Convention of 1864, Red Cross work really began in these islands in 1870 during the Franco-Prussian War, generous help being sent to German and French alike. That was the origin of the British Red Cross Society, which renders splendid service in many ways that even Dunant could not have foreseen, though he would certainly have approved of them. It applies first aid in accident and sudden illness, tends the sick in hospitals and their own homes, carries out welfare work for the disabled and handicapped children, and brightens the lives of old people and invalids. It has branches in many parts of the Commonwealth, the other parts having their own Red Cross Societies.

During the Franco-Prussian War doctors from the United States and from Britain served together in the Anglo-American Ambulance, and in 1881 the American National Red Cross was formed. While active in many other ways, it has a specially high reputation for disaster relief and disaster preparation, and for aiding servicemen, veterans (ex-servicemen) and their dependants.

In Britain and America the Junior Red Cross was organised during the First World War, and it also operates in many other lands. Thus old and young alike can help in this magnificent public service which Jean Henri Dunant began over a hundred years ago.

The Salvation Army

GENERAL BOOTH
(1829–1912)

For nearly two thousand years the Christian Churches have been trying to convert the world – to persuade its people to accept the Christian Faith. As yet they have not succeeded; although they have spread their Gospel into every land, only a minority of the world's people have so far accepted it, and many of those have done so half-heartedly.

Nottingham, where William Booth was born on 10th April 1829, was suffering from a series of disasters. Some time before his birth the town had been swept and flooded by a tempest; shortly after his birth there was a landslide; and when he was a few years old there were riots, serious crimes, disastrous fires and another landslide. The widespread poverty and distress which these produced made a lasting impression on his mind.

Yet 'Wilful Will', as the neighbours nicknamed him, was a cheerful lively boy, noticeable because of his long legs and his Wellington nose. He liked fishing and was a leader in his friends' games; when they played soldiers he was usually captain.

His father, who had once been well-to-do and had wanted him to receive a good education, had lost most of his money. Eighty years later William Booth well remembered how in his schooldays he had

had to accompany his mother on a business visit which involved a walk of eleven miles; the last mile, he recalled, took them an hour. When he was thirteen years old he was taken from school and apprenticed to a pawnbroker; he disliked this work, but his father could only console him by saying, 'There's money in it.' So William had to put up with it, compensating for having to toil in the gloom and poverty of the city by his walks about the countryside in his scanty leisure.

Plans for helping the poor of Nottingham were then being made, and young though he was, William Booth, whose work had made him realise their sufferings, was anxious to help. He had three ambitions: to make enough money now that his father had died to keep his mother and sisters in comfort; to be a political reformer; and to 'get right with God'.

The third of those resolutions was the most important, but at first he was hindered by a burden on his conscience. Some years earlier, when he had helped his schoolboy friends in some small business matter, they had thought that he had done so out of pure friendship and in their gratitude they had given him a silver pencil-case. As he had really been making a profit out of them, he now realised that to accept this gift had been dishonest. He did not mind returning it, but for some time he could not bring himself to confess his meanness. When at last he did so, he felt that he could now 'go in for God', and he resolved to do so with all his might.

That meant that he had to be zealous in his work and that he must devote his spare time to religious worship and to the service of others. He and a friend as whole-hearted as himself provided an old beggar-woman with a home and saw that she had enough food to live on – she was the first of the many outcasts who were befriended by William Booth.

Some time later, when he was seriously ill, he was revived by a message which his friend sent him: 'Get better as soon as you can. I've started some open-air religious meetings and we need your help.' After a little hesitation Booth was not only helping in these meetings but taking the lead in them, first singing a hymn and then addressing the bystanders who were attracted by the singing.

He had a way with young people, and while working with a group of poor boys from the Nottingham slums, he persuaded them to attend a nonconformist church, but when the minister and congregation saw these dirty, evil-smelling urchins trooping into the best seats they were taken aback and warned Booth that if he really must do that sort of thing, his followers would have to sit apart in the lowlier seats. The incident made him realise that he would have to conduct his services out in the streets.

At nineteen, when his apprenticeship ended, he went to London to look for work. Again he served in a pawnbroker's shop, his hours being so long that he had little time for his religious duties, but at last a friend who admired his earnestness offered to pay him a pound a week for three months if he would become a full-time preacher. Booth gladly agreed, and thenceforward he devoted his life to religion.

At about the same time he met Catherine Mumford, who was as earnest and devoted as himself, and who later became his wife. Even after their first child Bramwell was born, she worked with him, travelling round England on an evangelistic mission. Booth was so successful in this work that, although he had been equally successful when in charge of a church, he decided to become a travelling evangelist and to give up his duties as a minister. This offended the religious people with whom he had been working, so that he could no longer use their churches. In 1865 he and his wife decided to set up their headquarters in London, striving to spread the Gospel among the poverty-stricken people of the slums.

When people read 'Come and hear a Woman Preach' on the handbills and posters they were amused, for in those days such a thing was almost unheard of. Some of her audience had gone to hear the woman preacher simply out of curiosity, but when they had heard her they were impressed and stirred by her sincerity, and Mrs Booth began to be acclaimed as a public speaker.

Meanwhile, her husband was holding his own meetings in a tent – until it was blown down – in dance halls, and in a disused wool-store. He had to face much opposition, both from the old-fashioned religious people who did not approve of his methods and from the very irreligious roughs who threw stones and fireworks through the windows and howled abuse at the open-air speakers, pelting them with mud.

This discouraged neither him nor his wife, who combined her public work with bringing up a growing family. Although Booth was rather

strict with his children and particular about tidiness, they were very
fond of him, for he was kind-hearted and liked playing with them and
their pets. Yet the thought of the suffering in the London streets even
prevented him from enjoying Christmas with them and instead
the whole family went round the slums distributing Christmas pud-
dings – 150 of them. It is not surprising that Booth's health failed:
'Never again!' the doctor warned him, but six months later he was
working as strenuously as ever.

Helped by wealthy friends, Booth had founded the East London
Christian Mission. It still held its meetings in a variety of unusual
places and it also organised evening classes, reading classes and penny
banks for the poor, giving much help to the destitute and the sick.
Although it was opposed more hotly than ever, its work spread so far
afield that it had to omit the words 'East London' in its name.

The Mission was at first run by a Committee, but Booth did not feel
that this method was satisfactory so he decided to become its General
Superintendent and to take charge of it himself. In 1878, thirteen years
after he had founded it, he and his son Bramwell and another of its

members were preparing a report on its work. Soon he came to the question: 'What *is* the Christian Mission?' The answer was 'A Volunteer Army of converted working people' – for at the time the Volunteers, the forerunners of our Territorials, were much in the news.

Booth did not care for this, for he regarded his followers not as volunteers but as regular soldiers in the war against evil. Altering the word, he read aloud:

'The Christian Mission is a Salvation Army. . . .'

The three men looked at one another excitedly, for this was exactly what they were! And soon it became the Mission's new name.

This was not, however, the first time that it had been called an army. During the previous year, when Booth was visiting a Mission in Whitby, he found that he had been announced not by name but as 'The General of the Hallelujah Army'. About the same time, too, some of his followers had shortened his rather clumsy title 'General Superintendent of the Christian Mission' to 'the General'. Not wishing to be pretentious, however, he called himself not 'General Booth', but 'William Booth, General'.

The Salvation Army had not only its General, but also its other officers who were its full-time workers, for Booth knew that to have any real value it must be well-disciplined. Soon, too, it had its own emblem, the well-known 'Blood and Fire' flag of red and yellow, designed by Mrs Booth. It adopted its uniform rather more gradually, that of the women also being designed by Mrs Booth. Its Mission Halls were first called 'Barracks' and then 'Citadels', and its official paper was the *War Cry*.

Like the East London Christian Mission, the Salvation Army made use of singing, and some of its members could also play musical instruments. For open-air work brass bands were found to be most suitable, while many of the Army lasses accompanied the hymns with their jingling tambourines. As the Army had its own composers and its own poets, it soon had its own hymns, and its music was arranged so that bands from widely separated parts of Britain could join harmoniously in mass playing.

As in preparation for their services, companies of the Salvation Army marched through the streets in their trim uniforms, bands playing and colours flying, they naturally attracted much attention.

As before, there was often hostility; the old-fashioned people regarded these proceedings as vulgar, and the roughs who had persecuted the Christian Mission became more violent than ever.

Supported even by some of the publicans and the brewers, who realised that the Salvationists were urging the people not to drink intoxicants, and with no interference from some of the police and the magistrates, the roughs formed what they called a 'Skeleton Army', whose badge was the skull and crossbones. It interrupted the Salvation Army's meetings, destroyed its property, and assaulted its members, men and women alike. Sometimes it was not the roughs who were arrested and sent to prison but the innocent Salvationists whom they had attacked! Many unjust accusations were also made against General Booth, the mildest being that he was making money out of the Army by using its funds for his own benefit.

These attacks discouraged neither the General nor his followers, whose steadfastness was impressive and whose good work for the outcasts in the slums was beginning to be acclaimed. Public opinion was aroused; questions were asked in Parliament; the roughs became less violent and it was not the Salvationists whom the police now arrested. The Army became part of everyday life, and the wearers of its uniform were treated with respect. Even the toy-shops sold boxes of model Salvation soldiers, with their tambourine band, their 'Blood and Fire' flag, and a newspaper-boy selling the *War Cry*!

At one time attempts were made to unite the Army with the Church of England, but this proved to be impossible; instead the Church Army was formed, and although some of its religious beliefs and practices differ from those of General Booth, it uses many of the methods which he had devised.

While Booth always felt that the most important part of his Army's work was preaching the Gospel, he insisted that they must never neglect the poor. They ran homes for children and for the aged, provided shelters for the homeless, fed the hungry, and made efforts, often successful, to trace missing people; they tried to give renewed hope to people so desperate that they had considered suicide.

As early as 1879 its work had spread overseas, when a family of Salvationists who had emigrated to America founded a branch of the Army in the United States, and three years later two New York officers started another branch in Canada. In Australia two men whom General Booth had converted happened to meet in Adelaide and they formed a corps of the Salvation Army 'down under'.

Rather surprisingly, a demand for the Army came from Paris, and one of the three lasses whom Booth sent to take the flag across the Channel was his eldest daughter Catherine, who later took it into Switzerland. He was very concerned about this, for the Paris roughs had a great hatred of religion, but he realised that she had her duties and it was what she wanted.

In many of these countries, and in Switzerland especially, the Army had to face violent opposition, but as in Britain, this was at length overcome by the steadfastness and devotion of its members. There are few lands now where it is not carrying on its work, varying its methods where necessary to meet local conditions. In India, for example, the Army's pioneer workers wore the traditional robes which showed that they were holy men.

Regarding its work as a national service, the Army has never had any hesitation in appealing to the public for help. Like most of the other

religious bodies it takes collections at its meetings, and people who come along just to hear the band and the singing or through sheer curiosity are often glad to contribute.

In 1886 a Salvation Army Officer set an example which has achieved far-reaching results. When a special appeal was made for money, he handed up a slip of paper. Unfolding it, Booth read aloud:

'By going without pudding every day for a year, I calculate I shall save 50s. This I will do, and will remit the amount named as quickly as possible.'

'That's an idea,' said Booth. 'While we oughtn't to ask our people to go without pudding for a whole year, I don't see why we shouldn't ask them all to go without something every day for a week and give what it saves to help on our work.'

Following up this idea, the Army soon held the first of its Self-Denial Weeks, which brought in almost £5,000. Since then these Weeks have been held regularly every year, and the Self-Denial Fund has greatly helped the Army's work at home and overseas.

Early one winter morning in 1887 Booth happened to be crossing

London, and to his horror he found homeless people sheltering in holes and corners and on the steps of the bridges, trying to get a little warmth by covering themselves with newspapers and rags. As soon as he met his son Bramwell, who since 1878 had been his Chief of Staff, he questioned him angrily:

'Bramwell, do you know that people are sleeping out in this weather, sleeping on the stones?'

'Yes, of course, General. Didn't you know that?'

'You knew that and you haven't done anything! Go and do something at once! Get a shed for them, anything, so long as there's a roof over their heads and some shelter from the wind!'

Booth soon realised that it was not enough to try to convert people who are homeless and half-starved, nor even to provide rough shelter for a few hundred here and there. The problem was far too great for that; it ought to be dealt with on a national scale, but it would need to be carefully studied before anything effective could be done.

This task took him two years, yet he worked on it, despite increasing distress. His wife Catherine, the Army Mother, was suffering from incurable cancer, and after a long and painful illness she died in October 1890.

In spite of his anxiety, the General had meantime completed his book, and shortly after his wife's death it was published. Named *In Darkest England and the Way Out*, it shocked all who read it. Booth had discovered that there were in Britain at least three million unemployed, homeless people, worse fed than the lowest criminals in the jails. Most of them, he explained, had been born into conditions so hopeless that they would never have any chance of improvement; either they would take to crime or they would be condemned to extreme poverty for life.

The best way of helping them, he decided, would be to send them to work on the land in the under-populated regions overseas. But it was no use expecting untrained town-dwellers to be any good at farm work; they would have to be trained and, what was more, they would also have to learn to accept discipline. He therefore suggested forming three distinct types of Colonies.

There would be City Colonies where the townees would be given temporary work, and where moral and religious influences would increase their self-respect, and Farm Colonies out in the country where they would be taught to work on the land. When properly trained they would emigrate to Over-Sea Colonies which were to be large tracts of land owned and run by The Salvation Army.

Booth's Darkest England scheme attracted much attention, and though it was harshly criticised as impractical he received enough help from sympathetic people to carry out rescue work in the cities and to set up a Farm Colony at Hadleigh, Essex. His Over-Sea Colonies were never established, but instead The Salvation Army has sent about 250,000 emigrants to different regions of what is now the Commonwealth.

Apart from the attacks on his Darkest England project, Booth had many other criticisms to face; he was accused, for example, of being too dictatorial. He also had to deal with dissension among his own followers, some of whom left the Army. Three of these, to his great distress, were his own children; he felt almost as if this were desertion.

When he was nearly sixty he started to travel, visiting almost every country in the world, encouraging the regional branches of the Salvation Army and addressing public meetings to explain its work and ask for help. He found this extremely tiring, and the changes of climate and food told badly on his health. He especially disliked travelling by sea for the rolling of the ship and the continual noise wearied him, and it hurt him to see the idle, frivolous behaviour of so many of the passengers.

In spite of his travels and his work in running the Army he found time to write several books for its guidance. His *Orders and Regulations for Field Officers* reminded them that they must be an example not only to their own followers but to everyone. They must be natural and they must also be both earnest and cheerful, though avoiding silly laughter and idle jokes. Their uniform must always be neat, and except that the married women officers might wear a wedding-ring, they were not to adorn themselves with jewellery or other ornaments. Not only were they to abstain from strong drink – every Salvationist had to do that – they were not allowed to smoke.

Yet Booth made it clear that such prohibitions were not enough; the essential was that the Officers should be devoted to the Army and to the Soldiers they led, which would endear their Soldiers to them. They were to remember, too, that the roughs who still caused trouble at their services were the modern heathen whom it was their duty to convert; if the Army did not save such people nothing else would. They were to meet such conduct calmly and were not to let themselves be drawn into long, time-wasting arguments.

He also wrote Orders and Regulations for his Soldiers, and a book of religious instruction for children. The Army has always attached great importance to its work among young people, and has special sections for the different age-groups. Since General Booth's death it has formed its Life Saving Scouts and Guards for its boys and girls respectively; most of these now form part of Baden-Powell's Scout and Guide Movements.

So splendid were the achievements of the Salvation Army that in his old age General Booth became one of the world's most famous men. He had long interviews with the heads of other branches of the Christian Church and with presidents and kings, and when King Edward VII asked him what those Churches now thought of his work, Booth amused him by saying, 'Sir, they imitate me!'

When he was nearly eighty he found that his sight was failing, and he had to have an operation for cataract on one eye. The operation was successful, but some months later an infection set in and the eye had to be removed. Then Booth's remaining eye was affected; again he had an operation for cataract; again the operation was successful, but once more infection set in, and his son Bramwell had to tell him that there was nothing more to be done.

'You mean that I'm *blind*?' he said. Then after a pause he added, 'Bramwell, I have done what I could for God and the people with my eyes. Now I shall do what I can for God and the people without my eyes.'

In spite of his blindness he still worked, dictating his correspondence and his instructions to the Army. Even when his strength failed he was still as concerned as ever about the sufferings of the people at home and in other lands. 'Promise me,' he told his eldest son, who was to succeed him as General of the Salvation Army, 'to do more for the Homeless of the World. The homeless men. Not only of this country but of all lands. The homeless women. The homeless children. Oh, the children. Bramwell, *look after the homeless*. Promise me.'

When the promise had been given he seemed to be smiling as he added, 'Mind, if you don't I'll come back and haunt you.'

A little before the end he must have been thinking of the difficulties which a Salvation Army General had to face, for again he smiled as he told Bramwell, 'I'm leaving you a bonny handful!'

THE GENERAL HAS LAID DOWN HIS SWORD

So the newspapers announced to the world the death, on 20th August 1912, of William Booth. He was not, as might have been expected, buried in Westminster Abbey, although a memorial has been erected there to commemorate his work, but as his funeral passed through the City of London on its way to the cemetery in Abney Park, the traffic was held up for hours, not only by the thousands of Salvationists and others who were following the body of their dead General, but by the even greater crowds who thronged the streets to stand respectfully as it passed by.

In spite of its Founder's loss, the Army went on fighting as valiantly as ever against evil, and today his work is still going on in its meetings at the street corners, in its hospitals and dispensaries and clinics, in its homes for old people and children and in the help it gives to the poor. It is continuing in the Church Army, which uses so many of General Booth's methods in its own social work; it is going on, too, in the lives of the countless people who, perhaps without actually becoming Salvationists, have been influenced by the devotion and example of General Booth.

1906

THE CARNEGIE LIBRARY

The Proper Use of Wealth

ANDREW CARNEGIE
(1835–1919)

DUNFERMLINE, where Andrew Carnegie was born on 25th November 1835, had once been a prosperous centre of the weaving industry, but that was when the cloth had been woven on hand-looms in the weavers' homes. Soon after his birth, however, the new cotton-mills brought ruin to the home weavers; and among those threatened with poverty were his own parents.

Nevertheless 'Naig' Carnegie, as he was called, was a cheerful youngster who enjoyed even his schooling – until he found that his class-mates were calling him a teacher's pet. He had sound business instincts, too, for when he was only ten he and his brother made a profit by selling a large quantity of gooseberries in small deliveries from door to door. When he found that he was running short of food for his pet rabbits, he induced his friends to go out and gather dandelions and clover for them, promising that in return each of the boys should have one of the rabbits named after him!

When he was about twelve, poverty in Dunfermline became so acute that his family decided to emigrate to the United States. Young Naig was very distressed at leaving Scotland, and his first job was arduous and unpleasant, working a twelve-hour day as bobbin-boy – there were then no Factory Acts in America – in a Pittsburgh cotton mill for a few shillings a week.

His next job was slightly better paid but even more exacting; he had to run a small steam-engine single-handed, fearing sometimes that the steam pressure was too low and that the weavers would complain, sometimes that it was too high and that the boiler would explode. Even when he was employed as a clerk he was nauseated because he had also to dip the finished bobbins into vats of evil-smelling oil. Meanwhile he was chaffed by the other boys because of his small stature and his Scottish accent; but he simply replied, 'Ay, I am a Scotchie and I'm proud o' the name!' and he soon became as good an American as themselves.

When he got a chance of employment as a telegraph messenger he insisted on leaving his father, who had accompanied him, outside and applying for the work himself. He admitted that he was small and rather frail-looking and that he did not even know his way about Pittsburgh, but he asked to be given a trial, declaring that he would soon learn his way about the streets and offering to start work at once.

On being appointed, he began to memorise the positions of the principal firms and then the appearance of their managers, so that he could save time by handing their messages to them if he were to meet them on the street. As the work increased he found jobs for several of his friends and he was very pleased when they were all issued with trim dark green uniforms. When the other boys started quarrelling about who should take the long distance messages for which they were paid an extra fee, he settled the dispute by persuading them to pay it into a special fund which could be shared out at the end of the week.

While waiting for the telegraphists to arrive he learned the Morse Code and practised using the instruments by 'talking' over the wire to the boys in the other offices. One day when he was alone in the office and an urgent telegraph message came, he offered to take it down, 'so long as it wasn't sent too fast'. He was afraid that his employer would be annoyed, but when the man found that it had been received correctly he was very pleased.

Telegraph messages had first been recorded automatically on long strips of paper, which then had to be decoded by a clerk. Some operators, however, had learned to 'read' them simply by listening to the

clicks the instruments made,* and when Carnegie heard of this, he decided that he would do so himself. When the decoding clerk, who regarded him as a young upstart, refused to work with him, Carnegie simply stopped the recording instrument and took down the message 'by ear'. This impressed the clerk, who at once grew friendly, and people used to come into the office to watch Carnegie at work. Later he prided himself on being the third operator in the United States who could receive messages by sound.

When he delivered messages to the town theatre, he was often presented with a free seat in the gallery, which gave him a great enthusiasm for the drama and especially for Shakespeare, whom he read and re-read until he could quote fairly long passages from memory.

He was still anxious to educate himself, and when a Pittsburgh President opened his private library of 400 books to the town's working boys, he applied to be allowed to use it. As his application was refused because he was not an apprentice, he wrote to the local paper about it, with the result that all working boys, whether apprentices or not, were

* See *Inventors of the World*, page 88.

allowed to use the library. This demonstration of the power of the press gave him a great ambition to become a journalist.

Instead he remained a telegraphist, and his skill so much impressed Thomas Scott, Superintendent of the Pennsylvania Railroad, that he put him in charge of the Company's telegraph office. Here the eighteen-year-old 'Scott's Andy' gradually took over more and more of his chief's work.

One morning when Carnegie reached the office he found that a railway accident had produced an appalling traffic-jam, both the lines being blocked. Although he realised that he might get into serious trouble if anything went wrong, and that he had no authority to do anything of the kind, he started to send out orders in his chief's name. Fortunately nothing went wrong and when Scott arrived he was quite satisfied. He was equally satisfied when, after another serious accident in which several cars were blocking the line, he learned that 'his Andy' had cleared it by the simple plan of sending the terse message, 'Burn the cars!'

So Carnegie progressed and in 1859, when he was only twenty-four, he was appointed Superintendent of the whole of the railway's western division.

In those days sleeping arrangements on the train were very crude, some of the large freight-cars simply being fitted with bunks. So he was naturally interested when a stranger showed him a model of a contrivance which he had just patented, a 'seat and coach' car, the seats of which could be converted into comfortable beds. After persuading his chief to accept the idea, Carnegie took shares in the company that produced these sleeping-cars, the first ever built. They were very successful and paid him well, especially when, finding that another similar sleeping-car had been designed independently, he persuaded its inventor not to compete, but to co-operate with him in producing the famous Pullman Cars.

When the American Civil War broke out his work became of vital importance to the Northern armies, for the only line between them and the capital at Washington had been cut. Carnegie supervised its repair personally. During this work some telegraph wires knocked him over and cut his face so that, as he said, he was one of the first to shed his blood in his country's service.

During the battle of Bull Run he had to organise the troop movements by rail, including the conveyance of train-load after train-load of wounded. So arduous was this task that his health broke down, and in 1862 he took a holiday – the first he had taken since he began work fourteen years before.

Needless to say, he and his mother spent the holiday in Scotland where, in spite of a serious illness caused by overwork, he was able to revisit his birthplace and to do some sightseeing. On his return to Pittsburgh he was welcomed by an artillery salute fired by the local volunteers: the town had been expecting an attack by the Southern armies which fortunately never took place.

In 1861 Carnegie, realising that America was in great need of railway lines and engines, organised two companies, one to manufacture the rails and the other to build locomotives. Their motto, he proclaimed, was 'Make nothing but the very best' – and they always did. He realised, too, that bridges could no longer be constructed of wood. They had to be made of iron. He organised another company to build them, the first company in America whose bridges were strong enough to bear the increasingly heavy traffic.

Not only the railways but other industries were needing large quantities of wrought iron, and Carnegie started mass producing it in his Cyclops Mill, named after the legendary giants of old who were thought to manufacture arms and armour for the gods. Again he insisted that his company should produce nothing but the best and that it should always satisfy its customers; and he introduced a new 'costings' system to ensure that everything in the Mill was operated as economically as possible. This involved so much time and effort that in 1865 he resigned from the railway in order to give his full attention to his iron-works.

When these were in full operation he took a long holiday in Europe, not only visiting the historic places and enjoying the scenery but learning to appreciate painting and sculpture and good music. During the journey he actually descended into some of the volcanic craters – this seemed appropriate, for it was in such places that the Cyclops were supposed to have done their work!

In 1867 Carnegie left Pittsburgh to live in the business centre of America, New York. Though only thirty-three he now had an income of about £10,000 a year,* and he decided that it was not worth while trying to earn more. Instead he would spend two years arranging all his business affairs, and then he would 'cast aside business forever, except for others'. He would spend another three years completing his education and then possibly buy a newspaper and take part in public life. But soon something occurred to make him change his mind.

Hitherto steel could be produced only in small quantities, suitable for a craftsman. Recently, however, Bessemer had invented a method of producing it in bulk, and as soon as Carnegie, who was then in England, saw this working he realised its possibilities. Hurrying back to Pittsburgh, he astonished his partners by announcing, 'The day of iron is past. Steel is king.' Later he told them, 'We must start the manufacture of steel rails, and start at once.'

Finding that they were chary of supporting him, he started a new company and devoted most of his time not only to producing steel in bulk but to persuading the railways and other industries to use it instead of iron. He hand-picked his managers, driving them as hard as he drove himself.

'Oh, Bill,' he told one of them – for he was never a man to stand on ceremony – 'you don't know what a relief it is for me when I get on a steamer and start off for a long holiday.' 'Oh, Andy,' replied the manager, 'you don't know what a relief it is to us all!'

He still found time, however, to enjoy the company of well-educated men and to roam over the wild Alleghany Mountains, where he had recently bought a country home. Every summer he liked to travel, sometimes as far afield as Japan, or sometimes to the Scottish homeland that he still loved.

In 1881 he celebrated his success as a 'Steel King' by taking his mother on a coaching-trip round Britain – one of the old-fashioned horse-coaches, brilliantly painted, drawn by four 'noble drays' and with a coachman to sound his horn. The climax of the trip was his arrival in his home-town, Dunfermline, which was gaily decorated in his honour. Already he had presented the town with a swimming-bath, and now his mother laid the foundation-stone of the new public library which he was giving, the first of many such donations.

* There was then about five dollars to the pound, and both had much more purchasing power than they have now

Soon Carnegie, who was already head of the greatest steel firm in America, took over a rival firm; he also controlled a large company which produced coke, essential to the manufacture of steel. This metal had now supplanted iron in many industries, from barbed wire to battleships; there were steel pipe-lines, steel bicycles and steel-framed skyscrapers. The more steel was used, the greater grew Carnegie's wealth.

In 1887, shortly after his mother died, he married Louise Whitfield, a lady of thirty, and of course they spent their honeymoon in Britain. While passing through Edinburgh they stopped to lay the foundation-stone of a new library he had presented to the city, and when they reached their summer home a piper welcomed them appropriately.

Nobody could become a steel king without having to face difficulties and opposition, of which Carnegie had his share. His works were long free from labour disputes, but when they came in 1892 they were very serious – a strike culminating in such violence that the troops had to be called in. Unfortunately he was himself away at the time; had he then been in Pittsburgh the dispute would probably have been settled peaceably, for he was always just and reasonable in dealing with his employees. He would never employ 'blacklegs'; when he was faced with a strike he would simply shut down the works affected until it was over and the workmen were ready to return.

With his wife's full approval, Carnegie was anxious to make the best use of his wealth; as he explained in a magazine article, he felt it would be a disgrace for him to die rich. He was a charitable man and he fully realised the good work done for what was sometimes called the 'submerged tenth' or 'down and outs' by such organisations as the Salvation Army. Yet he, as he said, was 'not so much concerned about the submerged tenth as in the swimming tenth', the energetic and intelligent people who, given a suitable education, could lead really useful and productive lives. His aim was to relieve poverty by destroying its cause, ignorance, and he explained his schemes for doing this in an article written in 1889 and a book published in 1900, *The Gospel of Wealth*.

Naturally many people criticised him. Some thought that he ought to use his wealth to relieve the poor. Others wondered whether, as one of the wealthiest men in the world – he then owned several millions of pounds – he would really 'practise what he preached', but his only answer to such a question was, 'Wait and see!'

Even while making plans for using his wealth to the best advantage he increased it by extending his industries, improving methods of manufacture and finding new sources of raw materials. Faced with competition from another multi-millionaire, he settled the matter by making an agreement with him, and though he acted quite honestly, he got the better of the bargain. This put Carnegie in full control of the steel industry of America.

By the end of the nineteenth century, however, he began to tire of business life; he felt that he had made enough money and that now was the time to put it to good use. After some discussion, in 1901 he sold his industries to yet another multi-millionaire, J. Pierpont Morgan, for about eighty million pounds.

'Mr Carnegie,' said Morgan, as they shook hands to clinch the deal, 'I want to congratulate you on becoming the richest man in the world!'

A few days later he was dismayed to realise that he had nothing in writing; but there was no need for him to worry: Carnegie's word was 'as good as his bond'. When they next met, Carnegie said that he had made one mistake: he should have asked for another hundred million dollars (about twenty million pounds).

'Well,' grinned Morgan, 'you would have got it if you had.'

Freed from the cares of business, Carnegie spent much time in a new home which he had provided for himself and his wife and their only child, Margaret. He had been delighted with an estate overlooking Dornoch Firth in the North of Scotland, so he had purchased it, and there he had had a mansion erected. Skibo Castle, as he called it, was a strange mixture of Scottish and American, of ancient ways and new. Built of local granite, it was reinforced with Pittsburgh steel; adorned with battlements and towers like an ancient baronial castle, it had its own heated swimming-pool, and its own dynamos provided power for the electric lights and lifts. Above its topmost tower flew a strange banner consisting of two flags sewn together, so that the Stars and Stripes was visible from one side and the Union Jack from the other – a fitting emblem for the man whom the newspapers delighted to call 'the Star-spangled Scotsman'!

It expressed Carnegie's hopes that Great Britain would re-organise itself on American lines; as he explained in a friendly discussion with the Prince of Wales (later King Edward VII), he thought that the British Monarchy should be abolished. The Continental countries, he felt, ought to merge into the 'United States of Europe', but if Britain joined them, it would soon become completely insignificant. What he really hoped was that the British Isles would become States in the American Union.

Carnegie's personal life combined the traditions of Scotland with those of the United States. He seldom wore the kilt and never pretended to be an old-style Scottish laird, yet he continued the Scottish tradition of being a generous landlord to the tenants on his estate; he did not care for fishing and disliked hunting, but he enjoyed long walks through the magnificent Scottish countryside, and delighted in the bagpipes – even having them played at the fêtes with which he celebrated the American Independence Day!

Now the people who had wondered whether Carnegie would really practise what he preached were soon to be answered. Still convinced that the only way of overcoming poverty was to destroy ignorance and to spread knowledge, he set about providing the Anglo-American world with public libraries.

Already he had given one to his home town, Dunfermline, and another, as well as a museum, a picture gallery and technical schools, to Pittsburgh. Now he started presenting them throughout the English-speaking world.

Strictly speaking, he did not provide the actual collections of books. What he did provide were the expensive buildings in which the books were to be housed; it was for the communities themselves to provide the books, maintain the buildings, and pay the library staffs. He did not object when a building was described as a Carnegie Library; but he much preferred it to be plainly inscribed 'Free Library'.

Altogether, he presented nearly 2,000 library buildings to places in the United States and almost 1,000 in the British Isles and in what later became the Commonwealth. These were not only to towns in civilised regions but to the scattered outposts of the Empire, as far afield as settlements in New Zealand and Tasmania and the remote islands of the Pacific.

Carnegie not only presented many free libraries, he did much to advance higher education and scientific research. In 1902 he donated about two million pounds to found the Carnegie Institution of Washington, which has worked splendidly in many branches of science. The 100-inch giant reflecting telescope on Mount Wilson in California – until recently the largest in the world – was constructed, thanks to funds provided by the Carnegie Institution. In connection with its studies of the earth's magnetism, the Institution sent a specially built ship, the *Carnegie*, on a voyage of nearly 400,000 miles to check variations in the magnetic compass.

When King Edward VII was visiting his friends, the Carnegies, at Skibo Castle, he saw an unusual-looking sketch. It illustrated a prehistoric animal whose skeleton had just been bought for the Pittsburgh Museum. 'We must have one of those in the British Museum,' the King decided. Another such skeleton was not to be found, so instead, an exact plaster copy was made and it is now on display in the Natural History Museum, South Kensington. Most prehistoric creatures are named after the famous scientist who found or identified them. But this monstrous skeleton, that of the largest animal that ever walked the earth, is called after the millionaire who financed so much scientific work: it is the *Diplodocus carnegii*.

Carnegie had been deeply impressed on learning that during an accident in a coal-mine near Pittsburgh, a leader of the rescuers had died heroically trying to rescue the trapped miners. This led him to found the Carnegie Hero Funds in America and in most of the countries in Western Europe, endowing them generously, to provide a pension for anyone who had performed an act of heroism which had disabled him, or for his dependants if he had been killed. He similarly gave three million pounds, the Carnegie Endowment for the Advancement of Learning, to pension-aged university professors or their dependants.

Although he had become an American citizen, he had never lost his love for Scotland, and he had always venerated its ancient centres of learning. The Carnegie Trust for the Scottish Universities has done much to advance education in Scotland, by giving poor students fees to attend the universities, providing money for extensions to university buildings, playing-fields and students' hostels and supplying funds to endow new professorships and lectureships.

He still retained his love for his home town. In order to provide it with a park, he purchased a glen of great scenic beauty and founded the Carnegie Dunfermline Trust, whose purpose was 'to bring into the monotonous lives of the toiling masses of Dunfermline, more of the sweetness and light' by providing them with libraries, gymnasia, playing-fields and so forth.

He also founded the Carnegie United Kingdom Trust, with a capital of about two million pounds, the income from which was to be 'applied for the improvement of the well-being of the masses of the people of Great Britain and Ireland'. It has assisted art galleries and museums, fostered music and drama, built or improved village halls, youth clubs, family welfare and mothercraft centres; it has helped homeless families and handicapped children, as well as pioneering projects, nature conservancy, archaeology and other forms of scientific work.

Like all other thoughtful men, Carnegie was anxious to work for world peace, and he sought to bring this about by providing a Peace Palace at the Hague. He believed that whether there was to be peace or war would depend upon one man, the German Emperor, Wilhelm II, and thought that if the German Emperor and the United States President, Theodore Roosevelt, could be persuaded to co-operate, world peace might be obtained. When he proposed a scheme rather like the League of Nations for avoiding war, he suggested that the Kaiser should lead it!

This proposal failed, as did Carnegie's other plans for forwarding world peace. He could scarcely believe it when in August 1914 he learned that Britain had declared war on Germany, but he was quite willing that all the resources of the Skibo estate, down to the last of its magnificent trees, should be used in the country's war effort. In September he and his family sailed for America, and although he had now given away the greater part of his fortune, again he made generous gifts to promote education and science, to support such causes as the Red Cross, and to help individuals whom he knew to be in need.

When, early in 1915, the American President appointed an Industrial Commission to study the conditions of working-men, he gave evidence before it.

'What is your business, Mr Carnegie?' he was asked.

'My chief business is to do as much good as I can in the world,' he replied. 'I have retired from all other business.' Though at eighty years of age he gave his evidence very clearly on many difficult points, the effort tired him greatly. He lived another four years but never regained his strength.

He watched the progress of the war carefully, and was very distressed that his home at Skibo Castle was unsuitable for use even as a hospital – he would have liked to have visited it again, but in war-time that was impossible. He was amused when his secretary told him that during his life he had given away 324,657,399 dollars (about sixty-five million pounds). 'Good Heavens!' Carnegie exclaimed. 'Where did I ever get all that money?'

He died of an attack of pneumonia on 9th August 1919; but the wealth he earned is still being used by the various Carnegie Foundations, for the purposes which Andrew Carnegie wished.

The Boy Scouts

LORD BADEN-POWELL OF GILWELL
(1857–1941)

By modern standards, life early in the present century seemed rather dull. There were 'magic lantern' shows, and the first cinema films, music-halls, concerts and sing-songs; for those who enjoyed reading there were the free libraries which Carnegie had helped to provide and for the countryfolk there was the countryside. But townspeople, and especially their boys and girls, had little to do in their spare time.

There were of course boys' and girls' clubs, the Sunday Schools and the Band of Hope, but these were not very exciting. Perhaps the most adventurous thing a boy could do, if he liked such associations, was to join one of the Brigades. The first of these, the Boys' Brigade, had been founded in 1883 by Sir William A. Smith, and several others were formed later.

The 'B.B.' made much use of military drill, not to prepare boys for the Army but because it was thought to be good for their character; Bible-classes were held, for its real aim was to help its members to become good Christians; it gave training in first-aid, gymnastics and athletics; it had its own bands and gave public displays of its work.

The Baden-Powell family seemed to have inherited the adventurous pioneering spirit of their ancestor, Captain John Smith, one of the

Elizabethan Empire builders. It was certainly inherited by Robert Stephenson Smyth Baden-Powell, born in Paddington on 22nd February 1857 and named after his godfather, Robert Stephenson the railway engineer. Little Ste, as his family called him, was a brilliant boy, keenly interested in natural history and able to draw and paint skilfully – and with both hands at once.

At Charterhouse, the famous public school which he attended, he became a star performer in its amateur theatricals; when the school moved from London to Godalming he studied natural history and taught himself woodcraft in an adjoining copse. During the holidays he accompanied his elder brothers on adventurous cruises in their small yacht and on strenuous hikes across the countryside. In an examination for a commission in the Army he gained a high place, and in 1876 he became an officer in the 13th Hussars and set out for India to join his regiment.

He was efficient and popular, both with his brother-officers and with his men, though at the same time he commanded their respect; he delighted in playing polo and in pig-sticking, the dangerous sport of hunting the wild boar. While in active service near the Indian frontier he soon gained a reputation for scouting and accurate map-plotting, as well as for enterprise and courage, and he won rapid promotion. He also risked imprisonment by spying for Britain in several European countries.

Having served with distinction in a number of campaigns, he became a colonel, and when the Boer War broke out in 1899 he happened to be in command of a small South African town, Mafeking. He immediately organised its defences against the Boers who were besieging it, and though he was short of armaments and supplies, the methods he devised to bluff the enemy were so ingenious that the town held out until it was relieved on 16th May 1900, after a siege which had lasted 217 days. The results of this were far-reaching.

When the war began, the British had been confident that their soldiers would soon subdue a foe which they thought consisted of illiterate Boer farmers. They soon realised their mistake: though brave and devoted, the British Army was not trained for veldt warfare – and the Boers were. Faced with a series of disappointments and minor defeats, the British might have become discouraged, had they not been heartened by the knowledge that here and there some small British garrisons were still keeping the flag flying by holding out valiantly against heavy odds.

Their delight at the Relief of Mafeking is hard to imagine. The whole country seemed to go wild with delight; there were rejoicings everywhere, and a new word 'to maffick' was added to the dictionary. Foreign nations were amazed at this display of high spirits on the part of a people whom they had always regarded as dour and unwilling to show their feelings.

Already famous because of his defence of Mafeking, 'B.P.', as everybody now called him, became a national hero, and the British were delighted when Queen Victoria promoted him to Major-General, at forty-three, the youngest man to hold that rank. He helped to settle the guerilla fighting in which the Boer War ended, and in 1903 he was appointed Inspector-General of the Cavalry, with the prospect of even further advancement.

Yet promotion and fame did not satisfy him. He was becoming increasingly anxious about his country's future, fearing that, like the Roman Empire and the other great civilisations of the past, the British Empire might fall. Like many other officers he foresaw that the Germans might make war with Britain, and that even in peacetime our trade might be captured by the Germans – or the Japanese.

Worst of all, he feared that our people were beginning to lose the fine qualities which had made them great; our weakness, he felt, was 'bad citizenship'. He regarded our methods of education as being partly to blame for this; the schools, he thought, paid too much attention to pumping knowledge into their pupils, instead of trying to develop their character.

He was never a man to give way to despair, so he allotted himself the task of thinking out some way to restore to the British people the qualities which he feared they were beginning to lose. The problem was difficult but not hopeless, and he had several ideas on the right method with which to begin. He was already certain of one thing: little could be done for the older people; he would have to begin with the citizens of the future, the boys.

During the siege of Mafeking, the boys of the town had formed a cadet corps, and by acting as orderlies who would carry messages, keep on the look-out and perform minor duties, they had freed the men from such tasks and enabled them to join the firing-line. This made B.P. realise what splendid service boys could render, when properly trained and led.

He greatly admired the Boys' Brigade, but he thought that too much drill was a mistake; there were far more interesting and useful things which boys could do. He knew, too, of the good work done in America by a great naturalist, Ernest Thompson Seton, in founding the Woodcraft Indians, a movement which aimed at producing in boys some of the finest qualities of the heroic Red Men, as described in the exciting Westerns written by Fenimore Cooper.

When he was a cavalry officer he had compiled a training manual, *Aids to Scouting*. Part of this, he had been interested to find, had been reprinted under the heading 'The Boy Scout', in a weekly paper, *Boys of the Empire*, and boys and men had been using it as a basis for some exciting games.

So a plan began to form in his mind, and at last he was able to set it down on paper. He made some suggestions which he thought might be useful to the Boys' Brigade and possibly to some other organisations, and discussed them with friends whose opinion he valued. In 1907 he wrote a couple of leaflets under the heading 'Boy Scouts' and started putting his ideas into book form, but before completing it he wanted to see how they would work out in practice.

In July 1907, helped by the local Boys' Brigade, he organised a small camp on Brownsea Island in Poole Harbour, Dorset; it was attended by ten boys from the Brigade and ten from Public Schools. The boys, who wore shorts – unusual in those days – were divided into four patrols and were trained in tracking, stalking, woodcraft and, under a coastguard officer, in handling boats; they also played scouting and other games. Each patrol worked as a separate group, and each took it in turns to form a night picket and bivouac some distance from the main camp. Each was 'scouted' by the other patrol-leaders and B.P. himself. Every evening there was a discussion round the camp fire; the boys were taught self-discipline and put on their honour, a method which worked extremely well.

Indeed, the whole camp was so successful that Baden-Powell felt he could go ahead. In January 1908 he started publishing his book in six

fortnightly parts at fourpence each: it was called *Scouting for Boys*.

Baden-Powell began by appealing to his readers' patriotism: 'I suppose every British boy' (later this became 'every boy') 'wants to help his country in some way.' A boy could do this, B.P. explained, by becoming a 'peace scout', and for this he must train himself in wood-craft, in observing minute details and deducing their meaning; he must keep fit and healthy and be able to face hardships, and he must be guided by the ideals stated in the Scout Promise and Law.

To become a scout the boy must solemnly promise to be loyal to God and the King; to help other people at all times – which B.P. made practical by insisting that every Scout must do a good turn for someone every day – and to obey the Scout Law. The law declares that the scout must be honourable, loyal, helpful, a friend to all and a brother to every other Scout, courteous, a friend to animals, obedient to parents and Scout officers, cheerful, and thrifty. Later the Tenth Scout Law was added: 'A Scout is clean in thought, word, and deed.'

This might sound rather like preaching, but *Scouting for Boys* certainly is not. It does not read like a sermon; to study it is like listening to a kindly and experienced backwoodsman explaining woodcraft lore to newcomers on the open trail, to a fine man telling younger people how they can make the best of their lives. No wonder that it soon became, and has long remained a best seller. It has been translated into many languages and adapted for use in many lands; although it has appeared in over thirty editions, enlarged and in some ways revised, it is still unmistakably the book that B.P. wrote sixty years ago.

Baden-Powell had thought that his book would be useful to such organisations as the Brigades, the Y.M.C.A. and the boys' clubs, and perhaps also to employers and to schools. He thought it possible, too, that boys who did not belong to any of these organisations might form their own Scout troops.

Its results took him completely by surprise; all over the country boys started buying it as though it were something for which they had been waiting all their lives.

There were several reasons for its success. Westerns were just as popular as they are now, and at that time they were beginning to appear on the cinema-screen as cowboy films. Moreover, an exciting show, organised by an experienced backwoodsman, Colonel Cody, and unlike anything ever before seen in Britain, had been touring the country a few years previously. 'Buffalo Bill's Wild West' was a spectacular display by *real* cowboys and *real* Red Indians, of lassoing, rough-riding, bronco-busting and so forth, culminating in an enthralling sham battle between the ranchers and the Red Men, punctuated by the crackle of blank cartridges and by hair-raising war-whoops. With the memories of this still in their minds, it is easy to understand why so many boys welcomed the idea of becoming young backwoodsmen in real life!

Many of them at once set out, in ones and twos or in 'do it yourself' patrols, to practise woodcraft on the lines suggested in *Scouting for Boys*. Inexperienced as they were, and with no knowledge of anything resembling the modern Country Code, some of them became a nuisance: trespassing, leaving gates open, accidentally letting the cattle stray, allowing their camp fires to become uncontrollable, and – something which in those days some people thought was almost worse – playing truant from Church and Sunday School. Baden-Powell was startled to find that he was being held responsible for their escapades!

This was an unexpected problem for him, but he faced it with his usual determination, devising a scheme for organising these young would-be scouts. He set up a Headquarters office in London and arranged for County and District Commissioners and Local Associations to be appointed to supervise scouting in the different areas; an important part of their duty was to ensure that men who wished to become Scout officers were suitable for this difficult work.

Though the newly-formed Scout Movement was thus brought under adult control, it did not in any way damp the boys' enthusiasm; it simply enabled them to make the best use of it. They flocked into the troops and patrols formed all over Britain, and soon almost everywhere in the world; indeed, the only real difficulty the Movement met was that there were never enough Scout officers.

Scouting soon became part of the British way of life, welcomed largely because of the Scouts' cheerfulness and their readiness to help. The 'Scout smile' and the daily 'good turn' became almost proverbial, and the good turn might range from helping an old lady across a road to saving life at grave personal risk. No public event, from a Coronation to a village fête, seemed complete without its contingent of Scouts, running messages, showing people to their seats, doing odd jobs and standing by with their first-aid kits and water-bottles in case anyone should faint.

Tents and other types of Scout equipment went into mass production; poems were written for the Scouts, including Rudyard Kipling's *All Patrols Look Out*, and songs were composed for their use. Stories were written about them; the first, which is considered the best, being John Finnemore's *The Wolf Patrol*. The boys had their own weekly paper, *The Scout*, and their officers their own monthly *Gazette*. Books on various branches of Scout training were bought eagerly, but none was as popular or as useful as *Scouting for Boys*.

Busy as he was kept by Army duties, General Baden-Powell still somehow found time to encourage and lead his Movement; he toured the country – and later the world – inspecting the troops and addressing public meetings. Assisted by a small headquarters staff, he dealt with a growing correspondence. He wrote regularly in *The Scout* and elsewhere, some of his articles afterwards being reprinted in book form, and occasionally attended Scout camps.

Realising that this double role was too much for any man, he had to make an important decision. Had he stayed in the Army, leaving the Scouts to run themselves, he might well have become Commander-in-Chief – and then the First World War might have been waged more efficiently and ended more quickly and with less bloodshed. Instead, with the full approval of King Edward VII, who had recently knighted him, Sir Robert Baden-Powell retired from the Army in 1910 – though he was still on the Reserve – to devote his whole life to his scouts.

No longer known as the General but simply as the Chief Scout, he found that he still had a life's work for which he never accepted any pay. Scouting was developing in unexpected ways; it had spread across the seas, and even on to them, for the Sea Scouts had been formed. Experience had shown, too, that in some respects Scout training had to be modified and *Scouting for Boys* to be revised.

There was, for example, the Badge System. At the outset there had been only the Second and First Class Badges, with tests that would have seemed absurdly easy by modern standards, and four Badges of Honour, for signalling, first-aid, public service, and stalking (which, strangely enough, could be earned either by actually stalking an animal or simply by collecting leaves). Baden-Powell later added the Tenderfoot

and King's Scout Badges and the All Round Cords, with a Thanks Badge for those who had helped the Movement. He made the Second and First Class Scout tests more difficult and awarded many Proficiency Badges for a wide variety of subjects.

Accustomed as he was to surprises, even B.P. was taken aback when at the Movement's first rally he saw on parade a number of slouch-hatted figures wearing blue skirts instead of shorts; they proudly declared that they were the Girl Scouts. In those days co-education was almost unheard of, and he decided to form a separate girls' Movement, quite independent of the Scouts. Though keeping the same Promise and Law, they would be officered entirely by women, and they would have different badges and flags, a totally different uniform and name: they were to be the Girl Guides.

He found, too, that many younger boys wanted to be Scouts, but the training was far too strenuous for them, and the Scout uniform looked ridiculous on a small boy. Making use of ideas taken from Kipling's *Jungle Books*, in 1914 he formed the Wolf Cubs, with their own simple uniform and their own simple Law; he also formed another Movement, the Brownies, for the small girls.

Meanwhile, important changes had taken place both in his own life and in the world. In October 1912, he had married Olave St Clare Soames who, even after their three children were born, still gave him much help in his work. She became Chief Guide. Then in 1914 came the outbreak of war.

Though Baden-Powell, who as a soldier realised the horrors of war, had hoped that his Movement would help to bring world peace, he felt that every man should be ready to defend his country if it were attacked. Too old himself for active service, he wrote *Quick Training for War*, to help the recruits who flocked into the Army, and it was with his hearty approval that many of the older Scouts joined the Forces, and that those too young to do so volunteered for war work. In many ways they rendered valuable service; for example some acted as coastguards and others sounded the 'All Clear' on their bugles when the air-raids were over.

When the war ended he gladly returned to his original idea of using the Scout Movement as a means of encouraging friendship between the nations and thus helping to promote world peace. He arranged a series of 'Jamborees', international rallies of Scouts, the first of which was held in London in 1920, and at its end B.P. was unanimously acclaimed as Chief Scout of the World.

He had long been seeking some method of keeping boys who had grown too old to be Scouts in the Movement and also of attracting young men to it; he had already formed what was first called the Senior Scout Section and then the Rover Scouts. A similar Movement, the Rangers, was also formed for girls too old to be Guides.

Another project he had long had in mind, a camp where Scout officers could be properly trained, was realised when, in July 1919, Gilwell Park, on the edge of Epping Forest, was presented to the Movement. Here regular courses in various branches of Woodcraft were held, and Scout officers who showed themselves efficient were awarded the Gilwell Wood Badge. B.P. thought so highly of this work that when in 1929 he was raised to the peerage – rather against his will – the title he chose was Baron Baden-Powell of Gilwell.

He spent the rest of his life supervising his Movement, sometimes travelling far and wide to visit its contingents overseas, and continually having to deal with the many difficult problems which were bound to

arise in a changing world. Until 1938 he was still on the Army reserve, but in that year he retired completely to civilian life; he was worn out with overwork and his health was failing.

During the Second World War, as during the First, the Scouts rendered splendid service, but their Chief could take no part in this. With Lady Baden-Powell he had left England to live in another country which he loved equally well, South Africa. He made his home at Nyeri, in Kenya, and it was there that he died on 8th January 1941.

There has never since been, nor is there ever likely to be, another Chief Scout of the World. Yet in Britain, as elsewhere, there are regional Chief Scouts, under whose guidance the Movement is still flourishing: the 1954 census disclosed that it has more than half-a-million members, including over sixty thousand Scout Officers, in the United Kingdom. It is no longer world-wide, for most of the totalitarian governments have banned it, but in spite of this it has over nine million members in over a hundred countries.

Baden-Powell's influence spread far outside the Movements he had formed. It produced several independent scout and woodcraft groups which differed from the B.P. Scouts and Guides in various ways – some were not only co-educational but admitted older people and whole families, and some were quite small and did not last very long – but in their different ways they all did good work and there was room for them all.

As he had hoped, some of the ideas he had suggested in *Scouting for Boys* proved useful to the Brigades; and although he was aiming at world peace, they are also helpful to the Army, for example in the training of the Commandos. Adapted by the schools, some have become a part of modern education; the Outward Bound methods and those of the Field Studies Council plainly owe much to the work of Baden-Powell.

What is more, there are large Movements in foreign lands, and during the inter-war period there were others, which disliked B.P.'s ideals as much as he disliked theirs, but which none the less adopted some of his methods. The Fascist Balilla of Italy, the Hitler Youth of Nazi Germany, used to do so. The Pioneers of Soviet Russia and the Socialist Red Falcons of Western Europe still do.

Only a small proportion of the boys and girls who joined B.P.'s Movements ever became Scout or Guide Officers, Rovers or Rangers, but probably few ex-Scouts or Guides ever completely lose the effect of their training. It influences them throughout their lives, and they pass it on to others, some in their work in the Armed Forces or in education, but most of them to their families or friends. Thus it has spread to people who would never dream of joining any such movement at all. Thanks to Baden-Powell, townsfolk are much more open-air minded and like to go hiking or camping. It has been estimated that about fifty million of the world's present inhabitants have been affected, in one way or another, by his work, and even this large figure may be an understatement.

Under normal conditions his body would have been brought to England to be interred in Westminster Abbey but the war made this impossible. Instead he was buried near his home at Nyeri, within sight of Mount Kenya. In the countries which were then free memorial services were held; in lands occupied by the enemy those who mourned him had to do so in secret.

The stone which commemorates him in Westminster Abbey makes no mention of his Army rank or of his title; in the top corners it has the badges of the Boy Scouts and Girl Guides, and it bears the simple inscription:

IN MEMORY OF
ROBERT BADEN-POWELL
CHIEF SCOUT OF THE WORLD
1857 – 1941

'The Loneliest People in the World'

HELEN KELLER
(1880–)

BLINDNESS or deafness: it is hard to say which is the more dreadful affliction; and the lot of those who are both blind and deaf must be terrible indeed. How, we may wonder, can they ever understand or make themselves understood by others or obtain any happiness from life? Yet some, thanks to the skill and patience of their instructors and to their own courage and determination, have not only been able to gain an education and to enjoy life but to help others to do so.

Mr and Mrs Keller were, of course, delighted when their first child, Helen, was born on 27th June 1880, at Tascumbia, Alabama, U.S.A., and they were even more pleased when they realised how exceptionally bright she was. When only six months old she could greet people by asking, 'How d'ye', and speak and understand the words 'tea' and 'water', and before her first birthday she was able to take tottering steps.

When she was about eighteen months old, however, she was smitten by a serious illness; the doctors, somewhat at a loss, called it, rather vaguely, 'acute congestion of the stomach and brain'. Even when the fever left her she made little progress, and soon her parents realised, with horror, that she was completely blind and deaf.

Happily the illness had not affected her intelligence; when she was able to get about again she eagerly fingered everything in reach, inquisitive about size and texture and noting the slight vibrations which indicated movement. Anxious to convey her meaning to others, she succeeded, with her mother's help, in making some intelligible signs.

With her, as with other children, a nod meant 'yes' and a shake of the head 'no', a tug at somebody's dress meant 'come' and a push meant 'go'. To indicate that she wanted some bread she gestured as though she were cutting a slice and spreading it with butter, and she would give a shiver and pretended to be working the freezer to convey that she would like some ice-cream. Her mother could somehow make Helen understand her wishes, and it was through her love and sympathy that the child made any progress at all.

At five years of age she could fold and put away the clean clothes from the laundry and distinguish her own clothes from the others. She could tell by the feel of their dress when her mother or her aunt was going out, and make signs to show if she wanted to go with them.

Her violent fits of temper were more than ordinary childish naughtiness: she knew that she was somehow different from others and that distressed her. By feeling the lips of people who were talking she realised that they had some way, which she could not understand, of communication, but when she tried to make herself understood by moving her own lips she failed, and that made her furiously angry. Although, as she admitted later, she knew vaguely that it was wrong, she would kick her devoted nurse. Realising that this must have hurt the poor woman, Helen was sorry afterwards, but her sorrow did not prevent her from doing it again.

Her companion, a small coloured girl, seemed able to understand her, and they played together and did odd jobs about the house, working the ice-cream freezer, kneading the dough, eating scraps from the cake-bowl and feeding the hens and turkeys in the yard.

They wandered together round the corn-shed, the stable and the milking-yard, where Helen liked to stand with her hands on the cow's side enjoying the warmth of its body and the smell of the fresh milk, and she was not a bit dismayed when she got a hard blow from its tail. Sometimes she 'told' her little friend that she wanted to go egg-hunting in the grass, by simply placing her hands together and putting them on the ground, but she insisted on carrying the eggs home herself for fear her friend might tumble and smash them.

As Helen grew older her inability to make herself understood distressed her more and more, and her outbursts of anger became more violent and alarming. Her parents longed to help her but knew of no suitable school to which she could be sent nor of any teacher whom they could engage. Mrs Keller had read in Dickens' *American Notes* of a deaf-blind girl, Laura Bridgman, who had somehow been educated, but unfortunately the doctor who had instructed her was dead.

Mr Keller's inquiries led him to consult Dr Alexander Graham Bell, whose invention of the telephone had been an indirect result of his work in trying to educate the deaf.* Dr Bell quickly made friends with Helen and advised her parents to apply to the Perkins Institution for the Blind at Boston.

The teacher whom the Institution recommended, Anne Mansfield Sullivan, had at one time lost her sight almost completely, so that she understood the problems of the blind. She had moreover devised a method, based on that used in teaching Laura Bridgman, of educating the deaf-blind. Her best qualities were a kind and sympathetic nature combined with endless patience, and she could get on well with the young.

At first, however, she found her new recruit a difficult pupil. The child had realised that something unusual was afoot and felt uneasy and mistrustful, especially when a complete stranger arrived and tried to pet her. The stranger, she found, was kind but she was also strict; though she let Helen rummage in her travelling-bag and finger her clothes she simply could not be made to understand that what the girl really wanted was sweets.

Miss Sullivan wrote to a friend that though she had been expecting to see a pale delicate child:

> . . . there's nothing pale or delicate about Helen. She is large, strong, and ruddy, and as unrestrained in her movements as a young colt. . . . You can see at a glance that she is blind. One eye is larger than the other and protrudes noticeably. . . . She is very quick-tempered and wilful. . . . The greatest problem is how to discipline and control her without breaking her spirit. I shall go rather slowly at first and try to win her love.

* See *Inventors of the World*, page 95

She began by allowing Helen help unpack her trunk and by telling her, by signs, that the doll she found in it was a present. As this seemed a good time to teach her her first word, she spelled the letters 'd-o-l-l' into her hand, using a manual alphabet akin to that used by the deaf and dumb (the standard one-handed alphabet) which indicated each letter by the position of the fingers. Though she looked puzzled, Helen imitated the letters with her own hand, but she flew into a rage when the teacher took the doll away, meaning of course to return it when the lesson was over.

After similarly spelling out the letters 'c-a-k-e', Miss Sullivan made Helen copy them before giving her a slice of cake, which the child gobbled down greedily. Then again making her spell out 'd-o-l-l' she gave the doll back to Helen, who at once dashed away with it.

When next morning Miss Sullivan taught her how to use a sewing-card, she was delighted to see how quickly and neatly she completed it. Plainly there was nothing wrong with the child's brain! Hoping to teach her another word, card, she spelled 'c-a-', but before she could go on Helen had paused for a moment and then made her usual sign for 'eating'; those two letters had reminded her of the previous day's lesson!

Excellent pupil though Helen could be when her tasks interested her, she was still mischievous and whenever she was thwarted she lost her temper. Her table-manners were appalling: if she liked the smell of anything on someone else's plate or on a dish, she simply grabbed it. Miss Sullivan checked her when she did this and Helen flew into a rage so violent that her parents could not bear to stay in the room. After lying on the floor screaming and kicking for half-an-hour, Helen again tried to put her hand on Miss Sullivan's plate; when once more she was checked, she tried pinching her teacher, but in return for every pinch she was slapped.

With some trouble she was persuaded to eat off her own plate, not with her fingers but with a spoon, and it took an hour to teach her to fold her napkin properly. When at last this was accomplished and Helen was sent out to play, Miss Sullivan cried from sheer exhaustion.

After more of these struggles she told the family that she could do nothing in their presence, for they were so distressed that they tried to interfere whenever Helen made a scene, and this happened whenever she was not allowed to have her own way. They had to agree, though very reluctantly, that the two should be allowed to live by themselves in a summerhouse a little way off.

Helen was excited by the move, but on finding she was not to be allowed to go home she had another outburst of temper and it took two hours to persuade her to go to bed. Although by morning she had quietened down, she was still homesick and kept making signs that she wanted her mother. Finding her wishes thwarted she spent the day playing with her dolls and refused to have anything to do with her teacher.

When at last Helen realised that Miss Sullivan was kind and meant well she became more tractable and romped with her in the garden. She soon memorised a few words, as spelt by the manual alphabet, and seemed to know vaguely what they meant, but she did not understand how to use them, and she always seemed glad when the lesson was over. She also learned how to crochet and was very proud of making a wool chain long enough to reach across the room. Moreover, she let her teacher kiss her and would sometimes consent to sit on her knee.

When her father glanced in and saw her busy with her beads or her sewing-card he was delighted. 'How quiet she seems!' he exclaimed, for hitherto her restlessness had seemed almost uncanny. He brought her favourite dog to play with her and she tried to make it spell, in the manual alphabet, with its claws! So great was the improvement in Helen's character that it was soon possible to take her home.

After some weeks she could spell out nearly thirty words, mostly nouns and a few verbs; some of them she had 'asked for' in sign language, by patting her teacher's hand and pointing. As yet, however, they seemed to be only disconnected words, and she often got confused over the difference between 'mug', 'milk', and 'drink'.

One morning, while she was being washed, she showed that she wanted to know the word for water; Miss Sullivan spelled it into her hand. After breakfast they went to the pump-house, and what happened then is best explained in Helen's own words:

> Someone was drawing water and my teacher placed my hand under the spout. As the cool stream rushed over one hand she spelled into the other the word *water*, first slowly, then rapidly. I stood still, my whole attention fixed upon the motions of her fingers. Suddenly I felt a misty consciousness as of something forgotten – a thrill of returning thought;

and somehow the mystery of language was revealed to me. I knew then that 'w-a-t-e-r' meant the wonderful cool something that was flowing over my hand. That living word awakened my soul, gave it light, hope, joy, set it free! There were barriers still, it is true, but barriers that in time could be swept away.

Indeed there were barriers, as Miss Sullivan realised, for though Helen soon understood the meaning of a number of words and kept asking for more they were only detached nouns or verbs. She still had to learn how to combine the words to make sentences, indeed how to think.

Fortunately she had a cousin about fifteen months old who, although she had normal sight and hearing, was only about as far advanced in the use of language as Helen herself. Miss Sullivan decided that she would use much the same method of teaching Helen as was used with this child. She would 'talk' into her hand just as people talked into the baby's ears, and without keeping her mind fixed on anything too long she would try to interest and stimulate it.

Within a fortnight Helen not merely recognised about a hundred words but really knew what they meant. She did not as yet 'talk' very fluently with her hands and sometimes used signs to make her meaning clear, but she could follow the whole sentences which her teacher always used. Instead of just spelling out the words 'hat' and 'walk', for example, Miss Sullivan would 'say' in the manual alphabet, 'get your hat and we will go for a walk.'

She also thought it a mistake to try to teach Helen, or indeed any child, by playing infant-school games with beads or cards; the most effective way was to take her out and let her feel real things and to tell her about them. Educated in this way, Helen made wonderful progress, learning how to use adverbs and adjectives as well as nouns and verbs.

One day she rushed up excitedly to her teacher and kept spelling out 'dog-baby' on her fingers. One of the setters had just had five pups! This was a good opportunity for her to be taught the words 'small' and 'very small' and to learn how to count; for a time she was so enthusiastic about numbers that she started counting everything within reach.

Having obtained from the Perkins Institution some cardboard slips embossed with raised letters, Miss Sullivan taught her braille by letting her feel these with one hand while she spelled out the corresponding words into the other. After learning a few words Helen hunted them out in a braille reading-book; soon she was able not only to read quite fluently with her fingers but to enjoy a story or to learn something interesting, just as other children do when they read by sight.

Now able to talk on her fingers and to read braille, she learned as quickly as any other child of her own age – or rather more quickly, for she was unusually intelligent. Except for arithmetic, which she disliked, almost every subject fascinated her. She studied geography by fingering the raised clay maps which her teacher made, and learned about the world's early days by feeling the fossils which a collector had sent her, but the idea of those great monsters of long ago, whose uncouth names gave her much trouble, disturbed her sleep.

Even more than reading Helen enjoyed being in the open air, smelling and gently touching the flowers or climbing the trees. She loved animals, and when she was taken round a circus she fed the elephant with buns and rode on its back, shook hands with the bear and played with the monkeys. Though the 'many swift horses' rather daunted her, she stroked the lion cubs, unable to believe that such charming little things could grow up to be fierce. The performers gladly let her feel their costumes and follow their movements with her hands as they went through some of their turns.

Realising that what she really needed was the companionship of others of her own age, her parents regretfully consented, when she was eight, to send her to the Perkins Institution for the Blind. She was delighted to meet other children who could use the manual alphabet, though they seemed so much like ordinary children that she could hardly believe they were blind. She soon realised that she would have to work hard if she were ever to catch up with them.

She not only caught up with them but out-distanced them, and meanwhile she joined enthusiastically in their games and sport. For anyone blind and deaf it must have been rather frightening to be knocked over by a wave, but when she had recovered from the shock she enjoyed splashing in the sea ('Who made it so salt?' she wanted to know), or sitting on a rock and feeling the sea-breeze, the vibrations of the breaking waves and the clatter of the pebbles on the beach.

Spurred on by the company of the other children, she studied hard and learned to type and even to do ordinary handwriting. The Director of the

Institution was so impressed that he gave her much publicity – too much, Miss Sullivan feared, for she knew that overmuch attention can go to a child's head. She need not have worried: Helen never became spoilt; on the other hand, she felt it an honour that famous men should take an interest in her. Being told so often that she was wonderful rather bored her: what was there wonderful about learning when it was such fun?

Finding it hard to believe that so brilliant a child could really be blind and deaf, the doctors verified that Helen could neither hear the loudest sound nor see the strongest light. True, she could *detect* a slight sound, but only when someone was holding her hand; then she could feel the very slight involuntary movements of their muscles when *they* heard a noise.

Learning, when she was ten years old, of another deaf-blind child who had been taught to speak, she made up her mind to do likewise. Her instructress helped her by holding Helen's hand against her face as she pronounced the different letters. In this way Helen was able to put her own lips and tongue into the same position. After about a dozen lessons Helen learned to lip-read by touch and to speak. 'I'm not dumb now!' she exclaimed delightedly. Because she could not hear her own voice it was harsh. She soon realised this and was rather distressed by it, but still she preferred talking to using the manual alphabet, although she found that having an expert speaking on her hand was quicker than lip-reading.

When she was told of another deaf-blind child, a small boy, who could not afford to go to the Perkins Institution, Helen started a fund to help him. After her pet dog had died a number of people had offered to buy her another; she now asked them instead to contribute to her fund. The word went round, and so the boy was able to attend the Institution – largely through the generosity of America's dog-lovers!

To amuse her pupil Miss Sullivan had once described the beauties of the winter countryside to her, and Helen, who was now about twelve, wove them into a story so well written that it was published; then she was amazed to be told that this story had actually been printed several years before. Though she could not remember the story, it had in fact been 'read' to her when she was quite small, and in spite of its being forgotten it must have lingered at the back of her mind, and that was why she had been able to write it so easily.

In those days people did not realise what strange tricks the mind can play: unable to believe that she had forgotten the story, they accused her of deliberately plagiarising it. The committee before which she had to appear was so hostile, and the poor child was so questioned and badgered, that she became completely bewildered and did not know what to think. That night she cried herself to sleep, and for long afterwards the memory of this ordeal saddened her.

Her own family believed her, however, and so did Miss Sullivan, who encouraged Helen to write the story of her own life. This again was written so excellently that it too was printed – and nobody could accuse her of plagiarising that!

After two years' study at a school for the deaf, Helen, who had set her heart on a university education, entered a preparatory school at Cambridge, Massachusetts, first having to pass an exam in English, French and German, and in Greek and Roman History. Once at school she had to study more intently than ever, especially at her weakest subject, mathematics. Meanwhile she enjoyed the companionship of the other girls, some of whom mastered the manual alphabet so as to be able to 'talk' to her. She passed the preliminary exam for the University but then her health failed and she had to leave the school and put in an extra year's study under a private tutor at home.

One reason why she had chosen Radcliffe University, she declared later, was that they didn't really want her there. Certainly they did not go out of their way to make the examinations any easier for her. At the Preliminaries they had at least allowed her to have the papers 'read' to her manually, but at the Finals they denied her even this privilege. Instead the papers were copied into braille for her to read, but unfortunately several types of braille were then used in America, and some of the mathematical questions were in a type with which she was unfamiliar, yet in spite of this handicap she passed.

As at Cambridge School, she was delighted to be regarded as one of the normal girls of her own age – about twenty – and to join in many of their activities. Taking as much pride in her clothes as any other girl, she wrote home enthusiastically about her new party dress; she made a short speech at the class luncheon and was elected Vice-President of her class. She went with her friends to an inter-university football match and was very disappointed that neither side scored.

On the whole, however, university life disappointed her, nor was this simply because her disability kept her poring over her books while the other girls were enjoying themselves. She felt that she was driven too much and had to master unimportant details about the world's great literature instead of being allowed to appreciate its beauties; yet she would not give in, and after four years' study she graduated with honours, thus showing, as she had intended, that even a deaf-blind person could hold her own against those with full sight and hearing.

The wearisome grind at the University had not destroyed her delight in literature, especially in that of Ancient Greece, and she could always lose herself in a book. Using a special board and men, she could enjoy a friendly game of draughts or chess, or play patience with cards marked with the braille signs in their corners. She especially loved romping with young children, reading their lips with a gentle touch of her fingers.

She also liked long country walks and many outdoor sports: horse-riding, cycling on the back seat of a tandem, tobogganing and swimming; she rowed with oars firmly secured in the rowlocks, steering either by the scent of the water-plants and the bushes on the shore or by the feel of the current and the wind and waves. Strange as it may seem, she found canoeing especially pleasant on moonlight nights, for though

she could not see the moon she knew that it was there. She was as excited as anyone else would be when during an aeroplane flight she was allowed for a time to act as pilot, keeping well on course by feeling the slight movement of the controls.

While at the University she had planned to invite public assistance in founding a special school for the deaf and blind, but her old friend Dr Bell pointed out that this would set them apart from the world and prevent them from leading a normal life. As he advised her, she decided instead to wait until her education was complete and then to form an association aiming to give the deaf-blind special tuition in their own homes.

Assisted as efficiently as ever by Miss Sullivan even when the latter married and by another companion after she died, Helen Keller devoted her life to work for the deaf, dumb and blind; she served on official commissions and in many private societies sympathetic with her aims, and she travelled right round the world, striving to arouse the interest and sympathy of the governments and of influential people of many lands. She was present as an honoured guest, when the body of Louis Braille was interred in the Paris Pantheon, in 1922.

She was an enthusiastic supporter of many humanitarian causes, socialism, votes for women, the abolition of colour prejudice. Distressed by the two world wars, she pleaded earnestly for peace. Some of those who disapproved of her views but who had hitherto praised her courage and intelligence now altered their opinion: 'After all,' they said, 'she's deaf and blind, so what value could her opinion possibly be?' and when she appeared on the stage at variety shows to raise money for the blind, she was accused of making a public exhibition of herself for the sake of gain.

Everything she did attracted publicity; when she hoped to get married an enterprising journalist decided that a Helen Keller romance was hot news and announced it prematurely in the press, which led to so much unpleasantness that the engagement was broken off. Though distressed at the time, she afterwards drew comfort from the memory of this episode, for it showed that her fiancé had not wished to marry Helen Keller the celebrity, but had really cared for her.

Because she hoped that the knowledge gained would enable them to help other sufferers, she allowed what she called her 'scientific tormentors' to subject her to a variety of tests, some unpleasant and some actually painful. They found, rather to their surprise, that her remaining faculties were actually no more sensitive than was usual; they seemed so much more acute simply because, lacking sight and hearing, she depended upon them and so paid more attention to developing them.

Whatever the reason, their acuteness was amazing: when being driven through open country she knew whether she was passing open fields, trees, a house with a log-fire, or a printing-works, which she recognised by the smell of the ink. Incredible though it seems, her sense of touch enabled her to distinguish a red flower from a white one, to judge the characters of people with whom she shook hands, and to enjoy music and even distinguish the different instruments by the 'feel' of a radio-set.

In the intervals of her many travels she mastered several languages, read widely, and, using a special typewriter, carried on a large and varied correspondence with her many friends. She wrote a number of books interesting for their subject matter and excellent in their style, the best known being the autobiography of her early years, *The Story of My Life*.

Another of her books explains how much she owed to her religion: she was a sincere Christian, a member of the New Church founded by the Swedish thinker, Emanuel Swedenborg. It was largely her faith that inspired her to do so much for the disabled and above all for the people who, as she said, 'stared into the dark with nothing but the dark staring back at them', those who like herself were deaf and blind and whom she described as 'the loneliest people in the world'.

Warrior for World Peace

SIR WINSTON CHURCHILL
(1874–1965)

In spite of all the efforts made by Dunant and the Red Cross to humanise war it is still a terrible tragedy, especially since the invention of modern weapons. Those who fought to defend their country, therefore, did so to avoid worse evils, in the hope that their victory would be followed by a just and lasting peace.

Winston Leonard Spencer Churchill was born in Blenheim Palace, Oxfordshire, on 30th November 1874. His father, a statesman with a wide experience of public life, was descended from the Duke of Marlborough; his mother was of American birth.

Young Winston soon showed that he had an ingenious mind and plenty of pluck. Like many other schoolboys, he saw no sense in learning Latin; but, unlike them, he had the courage to say so. Naturally the master thought that he was being impertinent and threatened him with punishment; and, though he was only eight years old the poor boy was punished severely time and again, for discipline at that school was strict, but no matter how harshly he was treated his spirit was never broken.

His health was, however, affected and after a couple of years he was sent to a very different type of school, run by two kind-hearted ladies at Brighton. Here he was able to study the subjects he most enjoyed, English, French and History, and to ride and swim. He was still unruly in class and whenever he played with his friends he was always the leader.

When he sat for the entrance exam to Harrow School the Latin paper he handed in was blank but, perhaps because of his father's influence, he was admitted – though practically at the bottom of the class. He was so determined not to learn Latin or Greek that his masters decided that he was only fit to be taught English. He learned this very thoroughly, even winning a prize for reciting twelve hundred lines of Macaulay's *Lays of Ancient Rome* without a mistake! His contributions to the school magazine were so outspoken that the Headmaster threatened to 'swish' him, and as he did not excel at any sport except fencing he was not very popular with the other boys; not that this troubled him – he cared so little for their opinion that he did something which in those days was simply 'not done': he actually kissed his old nurse in front of them!

His father, Lord Randolph Churchill, was uncertain about the occupation for which so backward a boy might be fit, but when he observed the eagerness with which his son was setting out his army of 1,500 model soldiers in battle array, he asked him whether he would like to be an officer in the Army, a career for which a high degree of intelligence was not then thought to be necessary. Winston was delighted at the idea, but he failed twice before passing the exam which admitted him to Sandhurst, and even then he was rather low on the list.

To be posted to the Cavalry suited young Churchill well, for he loved horses. Enjoying his military training, he worked so hard that in 1895 he gained a Commission in the 4th Queen's Own Hussars. He was efficient in his duties, but his brother officers were amazed at his earnestness and his forthright way of speaking his mind. Peace-time soldiering did not satisfy him, however, and when a rebellion broke out in Cuba he went to the front. Coming under fire left him quite unperturbed, and he made his adventure profitable by acting as war-correspondent for a London paper.

When he was posted to India with his regiment he again became bored by peace-time duties, and even his success in playing polo, a sport he enjoyed greatly, did not satisfy him. Realising that his education was inadequate for one who hoped to be a journalist, he amazed the other officers by sending home for a supply of books and studying for hours on end. He read and re-read the historical works of Gibbon and Macaulay, the authors whose style he most admired, and upon which he tried to model his own.

When fighting broke out near the North-West frontier of India, he was permitted to go to the front as a war-correspondent, his courage and resolution being praised by the officer in command of the British forces. His book describing the campaign offended the Army authorities because it was too outspoken, but it was so successful that it induced him to write a novel, *Savrola*, with a political background. Though it sold reasonably well, the book did not fulfil his aims and he realised that writing fiction was not his vocation.

In 1898 there came a more important conflict, an Anglo-Egyptian Expeditionary Force being sent to liberate the Sudan from the fanatical Arab Dervishes. Churchill of course set his heart on accompanying it, and, despite the opposition of the Expedition's commander, Kitchener, he at last succeeded in doing so, as officer and war-correspondent. As he was in the thick of the fighting and joined in what was perhaps the last cavalry charge ever made, his description of the campaign attracted much attention.

He then decided to leave the Army to become a professional journalist, and to follow his father's footsteps by entering politics. He was a forceful public speaker, and was soon able to stand as a Conservative candidate in a by-election at Oldham. In this, however, he was defeated heavily, and his defeat was blamed on his youth – he was twenty-five – and his inexperience. 'I thought he was a young man of promise,' sneered the Leader of the House of Commons, 'but it appears he is a young man of promises.'

Unsuccessful in politics, Churchill returned to journalism. His book on the campaign in the Sudan had given him so high a reputation as a war-correspondent that he was sent by a leading London paper to report on the Boer War when it broke out in 1899. He was on his way to the front when the armoured train on which he was travelling came under fire and was trapped between some derailed trucks. As a war-correspondent he should now have been content to observe and report on the episode, but instead he took charge, freeing the engine and sending it, laden with the wounded, back to safety. Before he could escape he was captured by the Boers.

He was alarmed when his captors led him aside from the other prisoners, for he knew that as a civilian who had taken part in a military operation he was liable to be shot. He was greatly relieved when, instead, a Boer officer told him cheerfully: 'We are not going to let you go, old chappie, although you are a correspondent. We don't catch the son of a lord every day.' He felt, too, that the publicity this episode would result in would be a great help in his political career.

Life as a prisoner-of-war was so very boring that he soon made up his mind to escape. At the risk of being shot he managed to get away and, with a price on his head of twenty-five pounds 'dead or alive', he hid himself first under some sacks in a train and then, for three days, at the bottom of a coal-mine. At last, concealed under the bales of wool in a goods train, he succeeded in reaching neutral territory.

It was not long before he was again at the front as a war-correspondent. He took part in the relief of Ladysmith and in the capture of the Boer capital, Pretoria. Then, hearing that there was to be a 'khaki election' in Britain, he returned to England to take part in it.

Again he stood as a Conservative candidate for Oldham, but this time he got a tremendous reception as a war-hero. Nevertheless, there was so much opposition to the Conservative policy that he was elected only by a narrow margin.

Being a Member of Parliament was rather expensive in those days, and although Churchill had profited from his books he had to make some money by giving lectures on his experiences. He toured first Britain and then America, where he was announced as 'the hero of five wars, the author of six books, and the future Prime Minister of Great Britain'.

Four days after he had entered Parliament the new Member for Oldham delivered his maiden speech. Having denied that the British forces had committed atrocities during the Boer War, he pleaded for considerate treatment for the defeated Boers. His speech was received favourably; already, it was said, he was talking and behaving as an experienced M.P. This speech also won him the life-long friendship of one of the Liberal leaders, David Lloyd George, and it was partly through his influence that Churchill became increasingly dissatisfied with the Conservatives. Within a few years he had joined their opponents, the Liberals.

Realising his brilliance and his energy, in 1906 his new party appointed him Under-Secretary of State for the Colonies. This enabled him to help to reconcile the Boers with their British rulers and to form the Union – now the Republic – of South Africa. Two years later he became President of the Board of Trade, with a seat in the Cabinet.

In that year he met and married an American lady, Clementine Hozier. Their long life together was very happy; they had four children, and she always gave him the encouragement and sympathy he so much needed during his strenuous career.

During his Presidency of the Board of Trade, Trade Boards were set up to fix minimum wages and maximum hours of work in the various industries, and Labour Exchanges were provided to help the unemployed workers to find jobs.

In 1910 he was transferred to the Home Office. Having known the meaning of captivity, he became deeply interested in prison reform; he recommended, for example, that the educated prisoners should have a library and that all prisoners should have occasional entertainments to look forward to and reflect upon. One of his duties was to decide whether a prisoner condemned to death should be reprieved or whether the sentence should be carried out, and this responsibility weighed on him like a nightmare.

Early in 1911 some political extremists, one of whom had already committed a murder, had barricaded themselves in a house in Sidney Street, Stepney, from which they opened fire on the police. As anxious as ever to be in the front line, Churchill was soon on the spot, along with police reinforcements and a squad of the Guards armed with a machine-gun; he even considered sending for artillery or having the house undermined by the Royal Engineers. Conspicuous in his top-hat and overcoat, he supervised the operations, regardless of the risk of being shot.

Courageous though this action was, it hardly lay within the duties of a Cabinet Minister and, as a leading M.P. protested in Parliament: 'We are concerned to observe photographs in the illustrated papers of the Home Secretary in the danger zone. I can understand what the photographer was doing but not the Home Secretary.'

In the same year Churchill realised that Germany was seeking to rival Britain as mistress of the seas. Foreseeing the probability of a European war, he endeavoured to arouse the Government's sense of the country's peril.

He succeeded so well that he was appointed to the Admiralty, where he set to work enthusiastically to put the Royal Navy 'into a state of instant and constant readiness for war.' Working in co-operation with an experienced Admiral, Lord Fisher, he had the great battleships armed with 15-inch, instead of $13\frac{1}{2}$-inch guns to give the Navy striking-power, and the ships adapted to use oil-fuel instead of coal to gain greater speed.

Thus when World War I broke out in August 1914, Churchill had foreseen it and the Royal Navy was already mobilised and prepared for action. Again in co-operation with Admiral Fisher, he increased still further the size and striking-power of the Navy and made plans for its most effective use.

He also carried the naval war on to the land by directing the aircraft of the Naval Air Service to set up bases on the Continent from which they could attack the German Zeppelins, which were then threatening to bomb England, protecting the bases with armoured cars fitted with machine-guns. When the double line of trenches extended across France from Switzerland to the sea, he suggested equipping the armoured cars with a folding bridge to cross the trenches or, using steam-rollers, to crush them. After both schemes failed he proposed the use of what he called 'land battleships'.

Foreseeing that the trench warfare in France might last indefinitely, he worked out a scheme for overcoming Germany's ally, Turkey, by attacking the Dardanelles. The idea itself was quite sound, and had it succeeded it might have given Britain an early victory. Unfortunately, however, Churchill had failed to realise that combined operations would be necessary, and he persuaded the Government to agree to an attack by the Fleet alone. This was unsuccessful: not only were several of the ships sunk with much loss of life, but – worse still – it warned the Turks that another, more serious attack might follow.

The Turks at once started fortifying the coast, with the result that when an amphibious attack was launched they were quite prepared for it. After fierce fighting that caused very heavy casualties the Gallipoli campaign was abandoned as hopeless.

The failure was due partly to half-heartedness on the part of some of the war-leaders and partly to sheer mismanagement and confusion. Not realising this, however, public opinion demanded somebody to blame, and Churchill was made the scapegoat. He was removed from the Admiralty and appointed, as a sort of consolation, to the Duchy of Lancaster. Here, as he soon realised, he could have no influence on the conduct of the war, so he resigned and went to the Front in the rank of Major. 'An alternative form of service,' he explained, 'to which no exception can be taken and with which I am perfectly content.'

His fellow-officers at first received him very coldly, making it clear that they had no use for mere politicians, but his courage and efficiency soon won their admiration and friendship. Though he was promoted to Colonel, merely helping to win the war did not satisfy him: he still wanted to help direct it. After a few months he resigned his Commission and returned to London.

For a time he found that he did not seem to be wanted. 'I am finished,' he complained to a friend. 'I am banished from the scene of action.' Even the remembrance of what Lord Kitchener had said did not console him: 'There is one thing they cannot take from you: the Fleet was ready.'

Not only had he personal reasons for his distress; he felt that the whole war was being mismanaged. He could see that the Army's method of attack, a heavy bombardment followed by a mass advance of the infantry, was achieving nothing and resulting only in needless slaughter. The one practicable method, he realised, was the use of the 'land battleships', now renamed the 'tanks', which, thanks to his efforts at the Admiralty, were actually being constructed. He urged, however, that they should be kept secret and held in reserve until they could advance in large numbers all along the Front as an unnerving secret weapon; instead they were employed only in small numbers so that they lost their great value, that of surprise.

In his distress and frustration, Churchill was greatly heartened by his wife and by his happy family life. It was indirectly through this that he acquired a new interest: coming across a box of his children's water-colours he started to paint, and this so fascinated him that he at once bought an expensive oil-painting outfit.

After he had made a small blue mark on his new canvas he sat there wondering what to do next until a friend, the wife of an artist, happened to call. 'Painting?' she asked. 'But what are you hesitating about? Let me have the brush,' and she started painting with broad smooth strokes.

That banished Churchill's uncertainty, and he too began to paint boldly. The result so pleased him that he became an amateur artist, some of his canvases fetching high prices, not because they were the work of a famous man – for he submitted them under another name – but because of their excellence. He was not concerned about cash, however; he painted through sheer love of art.

In 1917 Lloyd George became head of a new Coalition Government. Wishing to include the best men of all parties, he soon found a place in it for his old friend as Minister of Munitions. Though this was much criticised, for Churchill was still being blamed for the Gallipoli disaster, Lloyd George insisted on appointing him, realising that his friend's energy and resourcefulness made him the very man to ensure that the Forces were supplied with the weapons that they needed.

When the war ended Churchill, knowing that because of our blockade the Germans were nearly starving, urged the Government to send them a dozen shiploads of food; he was anxious, now that their country had been defeated, to give it peace and sufficient power to defend itself. He was, however, very hostile towards the newly formed Bolshevist Government which now ruled Russia and he gave much support to the 'White Russian' armies which were striving to overthrow it. This made the British so uneasy – they did not want to be brought into another war – that Churchill was transferred to the Colonial Office.

Here his aim was to bring peace to the troubled Arab countries of the Middle East and to Ireland, which was in the midst of a Civil War. Though he failed to keep the southern part of Ireland in the Commonwealth he at least lessened its bitterness against Britain. He also checked the Turks, who were hoping to reconquer their former territories in the Balkan Peninsula.

Some of these actions made him unpopular. He again stood for Parliament in the election of 1922, just after he had had a serious

operation, but the result, he said, was that 'I found myself without an office, without a seat, without a party and even without an appendix.' In the two elections which followed he was again defeated, being howled down whenever he tried to speak.

Now banished from public life, he painted as a pastime and wrote as a profession. His history of the 1914 War, *The World Crisis*, was so excellent that its sales enabled him to buy a country residence, Chartwell in Kent.

Meanwhile British politics had altered considerably. Hitherto there had been two large parties, the Liberals and the Conservatives; the newly formed Labour Party was then comparatively small and seemed unimportant. Now, however, it became one of the chief parties, and it was now the Liberal party which was small and had very little influence. The election of 1923 put the first Labour Government into office.

Churchill hated Socialism, the theory that prosperity would result from nationalisation of industries. He believed, on the contrary, that this would ruin the country and he also feared that the Labour Government would try to introduce it. As he could see no future for the Liberals, he therefore returned to the Conservative Party.

In 1924 he was elected M.P. for Epping. The Conservatives were back in power, and Churchill was delighted when he was appointed Chancellor of the Exchequer, for this important post was the very one which his father had held years before. After a time, however, the Conservative Prime Ministers found him too difficult to work with and deliberately omitted him when they appointed their Cabinets.

Churchill now found a congenial task in writing the biography of his famous ancestor, the Duke of Marlborough, who, he thought, had been unjustly criticised by the writers of history. He worked very thoroughly, consulting experts on the period and travelling round Western Europe, where he followed all Marlborough's marches and visited every battlefield on which he had fought. He produced a biography so excellent that it might have been written by a professional historian, and in doing so he learned much about the art of war, many of whose principles have been unchanged in spite of the development of the modern methods of fighting.

By the time the book was published Hitler had come to power in Germany, and Churchill was one of the few influential men in Britain who foresaw a threat to the peace of Europe. The Germans, he could see, were not merely asking, as they pretended, for equal status with the other nations and the redressing of what they regarded as grievances; what they really wanted was revenge for the supposedly harsh treatment they had had to submit to after World War I. It would be easy now, Churchill declared, to halt their plans for re-armament, and then would be the time to consider redressing their grievances.

Instead the Government's policy seemed to be not only to allow the Germans to re-arm but even to encourage them to do so and to weaken the power of France. That made Churchill more anxious than ever; for centuries, he reminded Parliament, it had been Britain's foreign policy to maintain the balance of power by opposing any country which seemed to be attempting to dominate Europe, whether its ruler were Philip of Spain, Napoleon or the German Emperor, but Britain seemed to be deliberately abandoning that policy which had served us so well by allowing Hitler to make plans for conquering Europe.

As the Government seemed unwilling to take action, Churchill did so himself. He formed what was almost a private intelligence service to ascertain what was happening in Germany, getting information from unofficial people such as newspaper correspondents and refugees from Nazi oppression, and seeking the advice of experts. This enabled him to warn the House of Commons that the Germans had surreptitiously acted against the Peace Treaty, for they had built up an air force which was already very powerful and which was threatening to become even more powerful.

The Prime Minister, Stanley Baldwin, tried to soothe the startled House of Commons and the country by assuring them that Churchill was exaggerating, that the Germans were never likely to obtain as much air power as ourselves. Soon, however, he had to admit that he had been wrong, for the Germans openly proclaimed that their air force was as strong as the R.A.F. Yet, he declared, there was no need for Britain to feel uneasy; and the British people, still war-weary and anxious for peace, were only too ready to believe him. At the 1935 election Baldwin was returned with a handsome majority.

Again Churchill was left out of the Cabinet; this distressed him, not for personal but for patriotic reasons. As a Cabinet Minister he might have been able to induce the Government to take action against

Hitler before it was too late. He was not completely ignored, however; recognising his brilliance, Baldwin appointed him to the newly formed Committee for Air Defence Research.

Again advised by experts, some of whom were directing the research which later produced radar*, he made an intensive study of scientific air defence, while his contacts with the Admiralty enabled him to keep in touch with the progress of the Royal Navy.

In speech after speech, year after year, he strove to arouse the House of Commons and the country to the threat of German re-armament. It was not yet too late, he insisted, but if Britain dallied further it very soon might be, and future historians would never understand how after achieving victory over Germany in 1918, she had passively allowed the enemy to re-arm and to conquer her.

Neither the House of Commons nor the country was impressed, and Baldwin's successor, Neville Chamberlain, abandoned Britain's traditional balance of power policy and adopted one of appeasement. By agreeing to let Hitler have almost everything he demanded, Chamberlain hoped that the man would at last be satisfied.

Churchill opposed this appeasement policy for he saw quite clearly that the more Hitler was given the more he would want, as indeed, happened. When, promising that this would be his final demand, he claimed a valuable strip of Czechoslovakia on the grounds that most of its inhabitants were Germans, Chamberlain, supported by the French Government, gave in to him without even consulting the Czechs. This, Chamberlain announced triumphantly, meant 'peace in our time'.

Six months later the Germans had occupied the rest of Czechoslovakia and were plainly threatening Poland; then even Chamberlain could see that war was imminent.

War was declared in September 1939 when Hitler invaded Poland. At last the British realised the worth of the far-sighted man who for so many years had in vain been warning them of their danger. Almost at once the Admiralty broadcast a terse message to the Royal Navy:

WINSTON IS BACK.

Chamberlain had appointed Churchill First Lord of the Admiralty with a seat in the Cabinet and had thus put him in a position to help

* See *Inventors of the World*, pp. 161–175

direct the war.

During the winter of 1939 there were few land battles, and some people began to wonder what they were fighting for. 'If we left off fighting,' Churchill commented, 'they would soon find out.' He was furiously busy at the Admiralty, supervising such problems as the blockading of Germany, a convoy system for vessels crossing the Atlantic, mine-sweeping, the construction of new vessels, and the detection of German submarines and commerce-raiders.

Chamberlain seemed satisfied with the way in which the war was being conducted until in May 1940 the Germans overran Denmark and Norway. He then realised that neither the House of Commons nor the nation had any confidence in him so he resigned.

There was only one war-leader in whom both Commons and people alike had faith; public opinion, which once had scorned Churchill, now turned to him. He said later that when, on 10th May, the King had invited him to form a Government, he was conscious of a profound sense of relief. At last he had authority to give direction over the whole scene, which he believed, was the purpose of his life.

The whole nation likewise felt a profound sense of relief: here at last was a Prime Minister whom they could trust, a leader who could *lead*. They were not discouraged but heartened when he warned them of the hard struggle ahead and declared that he had nothing to offer them but 'blood, toil, tears and sweat'.

He formed a small War Cabinet, over which he presided as Prime Minister, and as Minister of Defence he also presided over the Joint Planning Committee for the three fighting Services, the Royal Navy, the Army and the R.A.F.

When the Germans had overrun France and Belgium, and the British Army had been rescued by the 'little ships' from the beaches of Dunkirk, Churchill was neither exalted at their rescue, nor dismayed that Britain must henceforth fight alone. He warned the people that 'an evacuation is not a victory'; but as he had declared in Parliament:

> We shall defend our island, whatever the cost may be, we shall fight on the beaches, we shall fight on the landing-grounds, we shall fight in the fields and in the streets, we shall fight in the hills, we shall never surrender. And even if, which I do not for one moment believe, this island or a large part of it were subjugated and starving, then our

Empire beyond the seas, armed and guarded by the British Fleet, would carry on the struggle, until, in God's good time, the new world, with all its power and might, steps forth to the rescue and the liberation of the old.

After the fall of France, Hitler waited for Britain to surrender. Needless to say, neither Churchill nor the British people intended any such thing. They were determined to struggle on alone and the whole nation responded to the words with which Churchill addressed the House of Commons:

> Let us therefore brace ourselves to our duties, and so bear ourselves that if the British Empire and its Commonwealth last for a thousand years, men will say 'This was their finest hour'.

Such words as these, repeated or transmitted by radio in and far beyond these islands, stirred the people not only of Britain but of the Commonwealth and the United States. Even in the occupied countries, too, people listening surreptitiously to Churchill's broadcasts at the risk of ferocious punishment, felt heartened, even though they might

not know enough English to understand exactly what he said, at the sound of his determined voice.

Fortunately Churchill and the President of the United States, Franklin D. Roosevelt, were on excellent terms, and it was largely thanks to this that America, though unwilling to be drawn into the war, supplied the British with the weapons and machine-tools which they so badly needed. Together, in 1941, they drew up the Atlantic Charter, a plan for the better government of the world.

This led Churchill to broadcast a message of encouragement to the conquered people of Europe: 'Help is coming. Mighty forces are arming on your behalf. Have faith. Have hope. Deliverance is sure.'

During the bombing of London which followed the Battle of Britain, Churchill would sometimes leave the shelter of his well-protected under-ground headquarters and insist on ascending to the roof to watch the aerial combat. When the raid was over the sight of the courageous people huddled together near the ruins of their homes moved him to tears, and he at once ordered a war damage scheme to be prepared to ensure that those whose lives had been spared were not threatened with ruin. In a few memorable words he reminded the people how much they owed to the airmen who had, as he said, 'clawed down' the raiders from the sky: 'Never in the field of human combat was so much owed by so many to so few.'

When in 1941 the Germans invaded Russia, Churchill, though his hatred of Communism had never lessened, announced, 'Any man or state who fights on against Nazidom will have our aid. . . . It follows therefore that we give whatever help we can to Russia and the Russian people.'

He did indeed give them all the help in his power, even sending large supplies of the munitions so badly needed by the British, through the perilous waters between Britain and the Russian port of Archangel. When the Russian leader Stalin pressed him to open the Second Front by invading Europe, however, he refused to do so prematurely. He always found the Russians very difficult to get on with. They seemed to have the impression, he commented, 'that they were conferring a great favour on us by fighting in their own country for their own lives', and he was horrified at Stalin's seeming contempt for human life.

On the other hand he and Roosevelt were excellent friends; they understood and agreed with each other's aims. Difficult and dangerous though travel was during the war, they met several times and kept in touch by cable and by their own private telegraph line. Their friendship became even warmer when, because of the Japanese attack on Pearl Harbour on 7th December 1941, America entered the war and became the ally, as well as the friend of Britain.

The war was now directed by the 'Big Three', Churchill, Roosevelt and Stalin. They met several times to discuss not only their war strategy but their war aims and their plans for achieving peace. Unfortunately Franklin D. Roosevelt died in 1945, to be succeeded by Henry Truman, whom Churchill hardly knew.

Even in the days when Britain had been threatened with invasion Churchill had been making his own plans to invade Europe, but he had insisted that the attack must not be made until it had every chance of success. When the Second Front was opened on 6th June 1944, he insisted, in spite of protests of the American commander Eisenhower, on taking part in the landing, and he refrained only at the personal request of King George VI, but it was not long before he was in France visiting the troops, just as he had already visited those in North Africa.

When it became clear that victory was in sight, the differences of opinion between Churchill, Truman and Stalin about the post-war world became more acute; and about the same time there arose differences in Parliament about Britain: Labour and Conservative Members were finding it increasingly difficult to remain united in a coalition government. On VE day, 8th May 1945, the war in Europe ended, and within two months Parliament was dissolved.

In the ensuing election Churchill did not, as many people had hoped, free himself from party politics and become a national leader in peace as he had been in war. Instead he had already become leader of the Conservative Party and in his electioneering speech he took even his own followers aback by solemnly warning the nation that a Labour Government would mean almost as much enslavement of Britain as a dictatorship cowed by a vindictive secret police.

Churchill, who had been applauded enthusiastically wherever he went, had failed to realise that the applause was for his work as a war-leader and not as a party politician. At first he had felt confident of again becoming Prime Minister, but during the night before the election he woke with a bitter feeling that he was going to be defeated. He was in fact defeated even more completely than he had feared, and a Labour Government was elected with a large majority.

His distress at his defeat was not on personal grounds; it meant the frustration of all his hopes for the future, the ending of all his plans. Hitherto he had been responsible for the whole future of the country, for its prosperity at home and power abroad; now his occupation was gone: he would have to look on helplessly while the Labour leaders grappled with the problems which he had meant to overcome, for he had no faith whatever in their ability to solve them. As he wrote towards the end of the first volume of his history of the War:

> At the outset of this mighty battle, I acquired the chief power in the State which henceforth I wielded . . . (throughout the) world war, at the end of which time, all our enemies having surrendered unconditionally or being about to do so, I was immediately dismissed by the British electorate from all further conduct of their affairs.

He still failed to realise that it was not he, himself, whom the electorate had dismissed but the Party which he led.

As regards foreign affairs, his forebodings seemed to be justified: at the conference held at Potsdam to settle the peace terms, the new Prime Minister, Clement Attlee, and Truman were inexperienced compared with Stalin. If only he had been there, Churchill must have felt, the post-war problems would have been settled very differently and much unnecessary hardship and suffering would have been avoided.

Although he felt that the people had failed him, he would not fail them. He believed that a little experience of Labour Government would make them turn to him, and meantime he could do valuable work as Leader of the Opposition, criticising the Government's plans and ensuring that they were considered from every point of view before they were legalised.

Although he was no longer head of the Government he was still honoured for his work during the war, for his knowledge of public affairs, and for his courage and integrity. He could speak for Britain in her dealings with the rest of the world, and his opinion always commanded attention.

The only way to preserve peace, he felt, was for the democratic countries of Europe and America to form a united front against Communism. On the one hand he urged the nations of Western Europe to co-operate, though he was not very enthusiastic at the idea that Britain should actually form part of a united Europe; on the other hand he was even more anxious that Britain should be more closely associated with the United States.

He did not wish Britain to become a republic and seek admission to the States, nor did he think that there was any chance that the latter would ever seek admission to the British Commonwealth! What he actually wanted was a 'fraternal alliance of the English-speaking peoples', involving not only friendship and mutual understanding but co-operation between their armed forces.

> I should like the citizens of each, without losing their present nationality, to be able to come and settle and trade with freedom and equal rights in the territories of the other. There might be a common passport or a special form of passport or visa. There might even be some common form of citizenship.

To increase understanding between the British and the Americans had long been one of his aims. Many years before, he had started writing a *History of the English-speaking Peoples* and he completed it at this time.

Throughout his disappointment over the election and his doubts regarding the future he was greatly helped and encouraged, as always, by his wife. He still painted for sheer enjoyment and wrote as part of his life's work. Years previously he had compiled a history of the earlier conflict, and now he wrote another similar work, *The Second World War*. Its concluding words show that he had at last lost the bitterness he had once felt over the result of the 1945 election.

> It only remains for me to express to the British people, for whom I have acted in these perilous years, my profound gratitude for the unflinching, unswerving support which they have given me during my task, and for the many expressions of kindness which they have shown towards their servant.

Affairs at home did not justify his gloomy forebodings, that the Labour Government would result in a dictatorship. Instead it produced the modern Welfare State, with the result that it was re-elected, though with a smaller majority, in 1950. In 1951, however, Labour was defeated, and the Conservatives returned to power, so that Churchill at last achieved what had long been his ambition – to become Prime Minister not as the result of a war-time crisis but by the free vote of the people.

In 1955 the Conservatives were again elected with an increased majority that showed how successful his administration had been. Just before the election, however, he resigned from the premiership; he was now over eighty and he thought the task should be undertaken by a younger man. He was still Member for Woodford, Essex, and though he was no longer in the Cabinet but only a backbencher his voice was always listened to with respect. Only increasing years and failing health made him retire into private life, still honoured and revered the world over, and especially in the country of which he was an Honorary Citizen, the United States.

He died, after a short illness, on 24th January 1965. For three days his body lay in state at Westminster Hall while by day and night more than three hundred thousand people filed past. Then, after an impressive State Funeral and a memorial service in St Paul's Cathedral, he was quietly buried in the churchyard near his ancestral home at Bladon. Almost immediately after the funeral his grave became a place of pilgrimage for those who still wish to honour his memory.

Monuments of Winston Churchill are to be erected within the Houses of Parliament and elsewhere. His home at Chartwell is now owned and protected by the National Trust, and that too is a place of pilgrimage for many of his admirers. The tribute that would have appealed to him more than any monument is the special Winston Churchill Memorial Trust, intended to provide travelling fellowships whereby men and women of the whole English-speaking world can extend their education and gain greater knowledge of the Commonwealth and the United States.

Yet the real memorial to Winston Spencer Leonard Churchill, artist, author, war-correspondent, historian, statesman and leader in peace and war, is the free world in which we live.